OIL ABOUT RANCHING

BY DENNIS McBETH

Page II

Front Cover Photo: Taken in the McBeth north pasture. After working drilling rigs in several states words cannot describe the appreciation (see Psalms 23:5) about getting a producing well on our own property. Recognition and appreciation to Tommy Davis and Joe Byrne who initiated the lease and first drilling and then sold the lease to lee Murchison and Willowbend Investments who developed and produced the lease. Small producing wells that are greatly appreciated. Cattle are being monitored and reprimanded by Frisco, a three-quarters border collie. It has often been said that the best livestock supplement is an oil well pump jack. The author agrees.

Back Cover Photo: Dennis and Audine accompanied by a Border Collie named Zebra and Quarter Horse named Charlie. Sitting in a non-authentic wagon which Dennis and son, Roy restored and that is occasionally pulled by two horses which they raised. Located at the entry of their place near Crews in eastern Runnels county, Texas which has been in continuous family ownership and operation since 1917.

OIL ABOUT RANCHING

BY
DENNIS MCBETH

Volume 1

COPYRIGHT: AUGUST 2015 ©
ISBN: 978-1-4951-7768-2

Published and Distributed by Dennis McBeth Consulting, Inc. All rights reserved and no part of this book may be copied or reproduced or rewritten without permission from the author.

To order additional copies e-mail: Dennis.McBeth@gmail.com

Printed by Ballinger Printing in Ballinger, Texas, U.S.A.

ACKNOWLEDGEMENTS

Many thanks to Bobby Frank, Steve Kelton and Paula Rankin at "Livestock Weekly" in San Angelo, Texas for making this possible. Also, thanks to Dr. C.A. Rodenberger who authors the column "The Computer and The Cowboy" and who made the suggestion for having a column about Oil & Gas and was the link who put it together.

A really big THANK YOU to all of the subscribers and advertisers of the "Livestock Weekly" and the encouragement that I have received from so many readers, many who asked when the columns were going to be published in a book. If you do not have a subscription for the "Livestock Weekly", get one for yourself and several for friends.

A powerful thanks to my wife, Audine (retired school teacher), who has tolerated this cowboy and oilfield worker for more than thirty years and encouraged me to try something new at the age when many people are thinking of retiring.

LAUS DEO

INTRODUCTION AND WARNING

"Oil About Ranching" originated as a column in "Livestock Weekly" in the spring of 2013 during the "oil boom". The goal of the column is to help bridge the information gap between ranchers and the oil field in an informative and entertaining manner. This is written from the perspective of one who has had his feet on both sides of the fence for many years. More than one reader has commented that when reading the column that it seems like we are having a conversation at the kitchen table. The unexpected blessing from writing the column is the many people I've met who immediately feel like old friends.

The columns and information contained in this book are not a journalistic endeavor but are written from the biased and opinionated perspective of one who has sweat equity in both industries. The purpose is to "stimulate awareness" and is primarily based on discussions that have taken place along with some good and some bad experiences. The author is not providing legal, engineering or investment advice and always recommends that readers make arrangements with appropriate professional advisers. The contents are much like coffee shop conversation and the author, publisher and all other associates and bystanders are not responsible for any ERRORS, Omissions or Distortions. Any and all definitions, formulas, formulas, statistics, market reports and other reference sources that may be contained herein are for exhibition purposes only and should be verified, authenticated, tested and proved by the user. Any and all appropriate disclaimers, whether stated or not, do apply and the decision to read this book creates an agreement that the author is "held harmless" and properly defended. This especially applies to any English teachers who might be drinking hot coffee and have a spasmodic reaction regarding the use/misuse of the English language. Some of which may be intentional. Due diligence has been applied to "keep it clean" and make it acceptable for a gift that you can send to anyone without need for apology, excluding English teachers.   One friend stated, "By leaving out the profanity from oilfield stories, it takes a third less ink and paper."   Please enjoy!

CONTENTS

    This book contains mostly columns that were printed in the "Livestock Weekly" in San Angelo, Texas between April of 2013 and August of 2015, except for the "rain poems" which have been added just because it seemed like the thing to do.

    The columns printed here are referenced by the prefix "LW" followed by a number instead of being numbered by chapter. There are some gaps in the numbering sequence because of using different computers and sometimes working on more than one column at a time. On occasion this resulted in some columns being being combined and others completed out of sequence and/or being submitted for publication out of order. Rather than go back and fill in the blanks, which would have put them out of order chronologically, the counter was re-set forward. It may not be the right way or the best way but, as is often said, it's the cowboy way. Look at the ear tags on my cattle to understand the logic. The sequence is somewhat in chronological order with the time line of an oil boom and bust with some information about oil prices and statistics along with some personal experiences.

Page X

Table of Contents

Acknowledgements V
INTRODUCTION and WARNING VII
LW1...Oil About Ranching...Be Safe 1
LW2...Oil About Ranching...Boom is On 4
LW3...Oil About Ranching...Break-even price? 7
LW4...About Ranching...Oil and Gas Lease…Spring 2013 9
LW5...Oil About Ranching...Fracturing 12
LW 6...Oil About Ranching...Customers" 14
LW7...Oil About Ranching...New Tractor in North Dakota ... 16
LW8...Oil About Ranching...Water 18
LW9...Oil About Ranching…Fracking 20
LW10...Oil About Ranching...Learning Differently 23
LW11...Oil About Ranching...Environmentalists 25
LW12...Oil About Ranching...Horizontal Drilling 28
LW 17...Oil About Ranching...Oil production in Texas 32
LW18...Oil About Ranching...Surface owner/no royalty 35
LW19...Oil About Ranching...reclamation 38
LW20...Oil About Ranching...Wyoming lease 41
LW21...Oil About Ranching...Economics of Production 44
LW22...Oil About Ranching...What is expected 47
LW23...Oil About Ranching...creation...9-16-2013. 50
LW24...Oil About Ranching...more oil production 53
LW25...Oil About Ranching...engineers & O-rings 57
LW26...Oil About Ranching...royalty taxes 60
LW27...Oil About Ranching...price controls 63

Page XII

LW28...Oil About Ranching...Hunting season warning 66
LW29...Oil About Ranching...Wyoming...Private property 69
LW30...Oil About Ranching...% of success 72
LW31...Oil About Ranching...resource info 75
LW32...Oil About Ranching...Oil price, rig count 78
LW33...Oil About Ranching...acronyms 81
LW34...Oil About Ranching...Thanksgiving 85
LW35...Oil About Ranching...diesel prices 89
LW36...Oil About Ranching...overrides 92
LW37...Oil About Ranching...Christmas, thirty years ago 95
LW39...Oil About Ranching...Cold 98
LW40...Oil About Ranching...cattle guards 101
LW41...Oil About Ranching...tight hole 103
LW43...Oil About Ranching...mohair 106
LW44...Oil About Ranching...pooling agreements 109
LW45...Oil About Ranching...production up 112
LW46...Oil About Ranching...Closed Loop System 115
LW47...Oil About Ranching...The First Anniversary (4-5-2014) 119
LW51...Oil About Ranching...Fence building 101 123
LW52...Oil About Ranching...Ear tags 126
LW53...Oil About Ranching...Peak Oil 129
LW55...Oil About Ranching...Well Control School 133
LW56...Oil About Ranching...renewable energy 136
LW57...Oil About Ranching...rig count up again 139
LW58...Oil About Ranching...read the document 142
LW59...Oil About Ranching...windmills 146
LW60...Oil About Ranching...sheep 149

Page XIII

LW61...Oil About Ranching...footprint & recycling 153
LW62...Oil About Ranching...July 4...freedom...pilot Don Orr 156
LW63...Oil About Ranching...Price dropping...snowmobile 160
LW66...Oil About Ranching...trash 164
LW67...Oil About Ranching...cattle and oil 167
LW68...Oil About Ranching...Prices Aug. 2014 170
LW70...Oil About Ranching...Royalty ownership 173
LW72...Oil About Ranching...drive by questions 177
LW73...Oil About Ranching...Hunting Safety 180
LW74...Oil About Ranching...Fracking research report 183
LW76...Oil About Ranching...oil prices   10-25-2014 187
LW77...Oil About Ranching...ethanol 10-31-2014 191
LW78...Oil About Ranching...fracking vote 195
LW79...Oil About Ranching...mules for royalty 198
LW80...Oil About Ranching...oil boom update 202
LW84...Oil About Ranching...Christmas 205
LW86...Oil About Ranching...chronology of the oil bust 208
LW87...Oil About Ranching...Analysts?...pound a year gain............212
LW88...Oil About Ranching...Lease impact. Cline. 1/26/2015 213
LW89...Oil About Ranching...oil consumption 1-31-2015 217
LW90...Oil About Ranching...holding oil until price goes up? 221
LW91...Oil About Ranching...Hendricks 225
LW92...Oil About Ranching...absurdities   2-22-2015 229
LW94...Oil About Ranching...rig to scrap yard 232
LW95...Oil About Ranching...oil inventories increasing 235
LW96...Oil About Ranching...Ag teacher and veterinarian 238
LW97...Oil About Ranching...timing 241

Page XIV

LW98...Oil About Ranching...methanol   (April 6, 2015) 244
LW99...Oil About Ranching...Texas Railroad Commission 248
LW100...Oil About Ranching...trail drivers 252
LW101...Oil About Ranching...Railroad Commission name change.. 255
LW102...Oil About Ranching...Production and Consumption 259
LW103...Oil About Ranching...greener on the other side of the fence 263
LW104...Oil About Ranching...Western Heritage 2015 267
LW105...Oil About Ranching...impact of oil prices. May 22, 2015 270
LW106...Oil About Ranching...damages & site clean-up 272
LW107...Oil About Ranching...production, consumption June 6,2015 275
LW108...Oil About Ranching...noise 278
LW110...Oil About Ranching...IRS 281
LW111...Oil About Ranching...break-even 285
LW112...Oil About Ranching...Maroon & Orange rigs 288
LW113...Oil About Ranching...Another look at OPEC's action 291
LW114...Oil About Ranching...heat stroke 295
LW115...Oil About Ranching...technology 298
LW116...Oil About Ranching...cold weather, warm dog 302
LW109...Oil About Ranching...Nepal 305
RESOURCES 308
Some Common OilfiField Terms 309
Common Oil Field Abbreviations 311
Needin' More Than Rain 313
THANKS FOR THE RAIN! 314
ABOUT THE AUTHOR 316

LWl...Oil About Ranching...Be Safe

Most of us do not appreciate anything that is written by someone who has no knowledge or experience regarding the subject. I do not claim to be an unbiased journalist and please accept that what I write about comes from the perspective of a broke cowboy who went to work in the oilfield in 1978 but never sold my saddle. It's a Donaho. Living on land (located in Runnels County) that has been in my family for almost a hundred years and having a small amount of oil production and royalty interest I do know how it affects my operation, my privacy (or lack thereof) and the bottom line.

Starting with "big oil" in 1978 I had a rare opportunity for training from several people who had extensive experience and knowledge. This began a journey which resulted in being a "company man" or drilling supervisor on wells in eight states. For those of you outside the industry, my job is similar to that of an on site project manager. Currently I work as a "drilling & completion" consultant. Since I am often asked questions about subjects on both sides of the fence, my goal is to provide some general information about the oil & gas business and the impact that it may have on landowners and local communities. (Disclaimer: I am not providing technical, financial, legal or any other privileged information and my opinions do not represent that of any corporation, person or this publication and all appropriate disclaimers apply.)

To say that there is an "oil boom" is an understatement for those living in the affected areas. Let's start with the most important issue and that is safety. My first close calls with disaster with oilfield equipment occurred before I was ten years old. Ignorance does not cause ulcers. I was unaware of the close calls that I had until many years later. We (my brother and some cousins who were all older than me) were out exploring in our pasture and saw a steel tank about ten feet in diameter that had been taken out of service and was laying on it's side. One of my cousins climbed up on top of the tank and sat down. Another one saw this as an opportunity to scare him so he lit a Cherry Bomb (that was a firecracker on steroids) and tossed in through a small opening. The Cherry Bomb exploded and the unsuspecting cousin perched on top was startled and we all laughed and went on with our exploring.

Many years later, I realized that it was a miracle that the tank must have been used only as a water tank. If that tank had been used to process or hold live oil, there could easily have been enough residual gas that the cherry bomb would have set off an explosion and nobody would have known what happened to five boys. We didn't even know we had a close call. No fear.

A neighbor bought some used oil tanks to use for grain storage along about this same time in my development. His son and I were the same age and we too were always exploring. These tanks had ladders which indicated that we MUST climb up on top. There we found a hatch opening and saw a ladder inside the tank which of course meant that we had to climb down inside. All we got was dirty. If there had been poison gas or even enough gas broken out of the old oil sludge to push out the oxygen, it could have been fatal.

Today it is even more dangerous because of automated equipment and higher pressures. Please, do whatever it takes to keep the kids, hunters and other visitors away from all equipment and facilities. Many of the pipelines laying on top of the ground are poly pipe and even a four wheeler should not be driven across these lines. If you see a problem please call the company contact and don't try to fix it yourself or shut it in. Remember the cowboy philosophy about drinking upstream from the herd and stay upwind from any gas leaks.

LW2...OIL ABOUT RANCHING...BOOM IS ON

In 2006-2010 Texas Oil production averaged (approx.) 342-369 Million barrels year. In 2011 production was up 19% to 436 Million and in the first 10 months reported by the Texas Railroad Commission is 429 MM with a projected (using monthly average) year end total of 514 MM bbls. for the year which is another 17% increase. 2012 production is up by about 44% over the 2006-2010 average. This production info was obtained at the website for the Texas Railroad Commission.

For those in the Permian Basin area of Texas, it is obvious that the oil boom is ON. I've seen traffic jams in Barnhart and Big Lake and hear that traffic is worse in the Midland-Odessa area. Many who participated in the previous big boom, circa 1980, claim that this is an even larger boom. Some of us who were herded out of the Permian Basin in the mid 90's were told by the experts with the big oil companies that it was a mature field that was on the decline and there was nothing new to discover in the area. New technology made a difference and evidently the new frac procedure can be very successful. It's exciting to see the resurgence, new life and excitement for something that had been ruled down and out. There are more "second chances" in this oil boom than were in the movie about Seabiscuit.

New life has been given to some old worn out oilfields. Some small towns are bursting at the seams while just a few miles down the road is another small town that seems untouched. Like the rainfall, the oil zones have an uneven pattern. How you are affected by the oil boom and your reaction to it probably depends on where you are standing. For people who want to enjoy lots of wind and sunshine, work hard for long hours, opportunity awaits. For a person who owns or leases a ranch with only the "surface rights" and no mineral or royalty interest, it can be a major inconvenience and disheartening to learn that the mineral interest takes precedent. One rancher told me that they treat him differently at the bank now that he has "money" in there.

Regardless of how we look at it from our individual situation, the surge in oil drilling has significant impact. It affects individuals and communities and that has been the case through history. I don't know the details but from what I've heard about Shannon Hospital in San Angelo and Hendricks in Abilene, their history is written in oil. We don't know how this boom will play out but history will probably repeat itself and there will be many educations paid for with oil money. Many new things will come and go. Some will stand the test of time.

From the rig floor, thirty feet above ground level in western Oklahoma, I could count 16 more rigs. Big rigs. Drilling deep. A supply salesman came by one afternoon and as we were visiting he made the comment as to how this boom was different and that we were in a different economic era and that anybody working in the oil patch "won't have to ever worry about another poor day." I sort of cringed and he asked whether I thought differently. My questioning reply was "You weren't in the cattle business in 1973, were you?"

That happened in 1982. The gas market broke and every one of those rigs was stacked out when they finished the well that they were on. The boom was over. By 1986 it was worse, when oil hit $9 per barrel. Many jobs and many businesses evaporated during the next few years. Some said that they would never go back to the oilfield. There's a new crop of hands with youthful exuberance and excitement. They ask me if I think that this boom will end and when. My reply: "Yes but I don't know when. Dave Ramsey is right---pay cash."

I'm back in for another go round. Like a typical cowboy deal, I did not agree to go to work full time. The call in mid December 2011 was to just come help out for a few days. Plan on being on site four to eight days. I worked 13 days in December, 27 in January and then it got real busy.

LW3...Oil About Ranching...Break-even Price?

There is probably no need to be concerned about overstating the obvious when saying that there is an oil boom in Texas and a few other states. This affects all of us as consumers and taxpayers. Our perspective is usually based on how we are directly impacted. Growing up in the country and raising livestock I am connected to the land and live on a small piece of property that has been in my family for almost one hundred years. Having been a broke cowboy who went to work in the oilfield, I am glad that I had the opportunity to meet Elmer Kelton shortly after I read his book "Honor At Daybreak" about the early oilfield and tell him how much I could identify with some of the characters and situations.

As a landowner, royalty owner and a drilling consultant I have my feet on both sides of the fence and often I am asked about technical, economic and other general information questions. Hopefully, through healthy discussions we can all become more knowledgeable and more aware of the activity around us and the impact that it may have on different individuals.

Often I am quizzed about oil prices being so high and then wanting to know the break even price for oil. Determining the break-even price for oil is like saying at what price cattle are cattle profitable. The ideal cattle situation might be some strong grass country, with no mortgage and low taxes, with twenty pastures set up in a rotational grazing system, no poisonous or invasive plant species, a healthy closed herd system with just the right amount of rainfall, and buyers who pay a premium to buy the calves directly off the ranch. To an observer, it looks like it's nearly all pure profit but to the man who just finished paying off the mortgage and has spent years building fences, doing conservation work and building a solid breeding herd, he is looking at a small single digit return on his investment.

Like the rancher, each oil company has it's own scenario and history and that is probably different on each lease where they operate. The casual observer often makes a statement to the effect that if they were making money at $40 oil then they should be getting rich at $90 per barrel oil. Apply a similar question using eighty cent calves a few years ago compared to $1.50 per pound now. Both situations involve all of the changes pertaining to input costs for the production. When you consider taxes, taxes (yes I'm being redundant but so are taxes), labor, fuel, insurance, losses, disasters and any other number of things, it is and almost always has been a challenge to make a profit in ranching, oil or any other business.

I don't have privilege to any company's financial data and don't know the targeted projections but do know that there is a sense of optimism in the oilfield when prices are more than $100 per barrel and I remember the panic and project cancellations that occurred when oil dropped to $40 in 2008. The long range question is not the break even price but at what price will exploration and development continue. Just as the price of calves is dependent on investors putting them in the feed yard, the development of new wells and use of new technology is dependent on those who are willing to take the risk.

LW4...About Ranching...Oil and Gas Lease Spring 2013

Before the drilling begins, there must be a lease for the property. (Every situation is different so consult an attorney. This is merely a glimpse of a few thoughts for discussion purposes and all appropriate disclaimers apply.) An offer for a lease may come directly from an oil company, an agent acting on behalf of an oil company or an investor who is planning to sell the lease to another party at some later date. I have been reminded many times that "what's signed matters and what's said doesn't".

The terms of a lease may involve a time period which specifies a date by which drilling operations must begin and a production clause that the lease is in force for as long as there is any production of oil or gas coming from that lease. There may be a clause for the operator to have a specified time even after production has stopped. This could allow the operator time to drill another well and or do some enhanced recovery operations.

I am aware of one lease that has been in place for about sixty years and have a royalty check for $55 to prove it. This also indicates that all royalty owners are not rich. It's also proof that being thankful and appreciative may not be based on, or limited by the amount. A lease may be in place for a long time and may impact a few generations in a family. Some of us with a farm and ranch background may mistakenly think of a two year oil & gas lease similar to how we think of a two year grass lease instead of thinking about the long term implications.

It would have been much simpler if the surface ownership and the mineral ownership below the surface had never been divided. Many people living on small acreage tracts in sub-divisions have been surprised to see a drilling rig move into the neighborhood and learn something to the effect that mineral rights take precedence and that the company with a lease does have a right to drill in that area with various stipulations and limitations, as the case may be.

As I look at it from the position of a surface owner with a partial mineral interest who also lives on the property, I had some definite priorities. I wanted to lease to the same operator who had drilled and was producing some wells just across the fence. I've worked as a drilling supervisor in eight states and my opinion is that just about anybody can drill a well but what really counts is whether an operator knows how to produce in that area. Not much different from share cropping a cotton field. But there is always the exception that a new player may be much more aggressive and work harder. To me, in that situation, my number one priority was about having an operator with proven production capabilities. The dollar amount per acre was a low priority.

Since I live on the property, I wanted to be specific regarding minimum distances for roads and locations in proximity to our house. As much appreciation as I have for their efforts, I still don't want all the traffic going by my front door. With that in mind, I am also aware that 660' is very close proximity for a drilling rig and that if a location is built that close to the house, we may prefer temporary housing in town.

In the long term, I have seen evidence, that wildlife

will adjust to oil and gas operations. In the short term it may mess up your hunting and a specified hunting season exclusion may be considered. Circle pivot and other irrigation systems cause other concerns. It's always good to make a list of priorities and concerns. Damage payments for roads, locations, pipelines and other facilities need to be specific and if a surface lessor is involved, it needs to be specified whether the landowner, lessor or a designated agent is to negotiate for damages and to whom damages will be paid. An important part of any contract is to prevent confusion in the future.

Rumors are plentiful about the leasing activity in some of the areas where drilling is anticipated. I'm reminded of the investment cliché to sell the rumor and buy the fact. We can only read about the Gold Rush of 1849 but some of us can see this current oil boom up close. Several years ago, after reading the book Honor At Daybreak, I met the author, the late Mr. Elmer Kelton. I'm glad that I had the opportunity to tell him how closely that I identified with the line by one of the characters who said something to the effect that he hadn't gotten rich in the oilfield like some had done but that he had a ringside seat to one of the greatest shows on earth.

LW5...OIL ABOUT RANCHING...FRACTURING

(Cowboy Answers to some oilfield questions. All applicable disclaimers apply!)

Does "fracking" damage the fresh water zone? That is a question that I hear very often and it is a valid concern. The question is then often followed with a statement questioning whether those who are doing the frac job care whether or not a water zone is damaged. This re-positions the question from science to emotion with the burden of proof being able to support the argument as to whether someone "cares".

In time I hope to give more info regarding the frac process and pressure gradients, zone isolation and formation permeability. When a person's mind is made up based on their emotional reaction, there is nothing to be gained by confusing them with the facts. To give a short and simple answer to a question about a complicated process is always a challenge. A simple way to look at hydraulic fracturing is to use the hydraulic bottle jack as an example. If you've ever used a hydraulic jack, it is obvious that a relatively small amount of energy (arm movement on a lever) can be used to lift the axle of a heavy trailer. If you've ever used one of these jacks that has a leak, the axle will not be lifted.

Take this concept and then "follow the money". If the frac fluid is not controlled and delivered to the desired zone, it is a total waste. It's a little like what I learned at an early age using Dr. Roger's Phenothiazine sheep drench; getting a dose of it all over my arm instead of down the ewe's throat was an undesirable outcome. When attempting to frac a zone at 5,000' the normal pressure gradient may be slightly over 2,100 pounds per square inch (psi). The water zone at 300' depth may have a normal pressure gradient of 130 psi.

If there is communication (a transfer of pressure and volume) from the desired zone to a lower pressured zone, the frac job will be a complete failure. Similar to the leaking hydraulic jack, all the effort is wasted. Hydraulic pressure will follow the path of least resistance. For a successful frac job, the force must be directed and controlled into the desired zone. With a few million dollars invested, it is imperative that the frac job be done correctly. The frac jobs are very well engineered and state of the art technology. The jobs of the people involved are dependent upon them doing it correctly. The reality is that the oil companies have a vested financial interest in doing the frac job in the right way.

LW 6...OIL ABOUT RANCHING...CUSTOMERS

Ranchers best customers often wear hard hats and steel toed boots. Sometimes I fail to see the obvious but it was brought to my attention this week while on a drilling location. The idea was that it sure would be nice to go eat a good steak but just didn't have the time. That is true with many people who are working long hours, but when they do have some time off, they are the most likely customer for a big steak or a double meat hamburger. The hard working individual who is putting in so much overtime that he doesn't have much time to clean up is also the one who is also making more money than ever before. There's the perfect customer; hungry and with money to spend.

A few weeks ago I met a real chef who had just catered a big fajita feast for the crew on a frac job. I wasn't on site but got to eat some leftovers. No doubt those exceptional fajitas were appreciated by all the hands on that job. This man is a real chef who has developed some of his own seasonings and is marketing them through some big stores and on the internet. More than simply a cook, he approaches the task much like an artist or craftsman and wants the next meal to be better than the one before.

Stories about chuck wagon cooks came to mind about how some hands would stay or leave because of the wagon cook. Hardworking people always appreciate a good meal. In the oilpatch, like many other places, a good steak is usually considered to be the best meal and everything else falls into line somewhere below. As the conversation turns to what they are going to do on their days off, very often it is focused around cooking some steaks and burgers on the grill.

Maybe he's a roughneck, truck driver, welder, cementer or frac hand, regardless of his unkempt appearance, just remember that from a beef producer's viewpoint that guy is a CUSTOMER. So when we get frustrated by all of this oilfield traffic and we see these people in the stores who haven't had the time or opportunity to clean up, we need to smile and remember that individual is probably a very good beef customer.

LW7...Oil About Ranching...New Tractor in North Dakota

A drilling consultant who had worked in North Dakota told me that they drilled some high producing wells on a farm there and that the farmer had suddenly become rich. Then he asked, "Do you know what that farmer did?" and without waiting for me to answer, he proclaimed with astonishment, "He bought a NEW TRACTOR!"

I'm sitting there thinking "well, yeah, that's exactly what would be expected." He went on to say that with all that money that the farmer could have gotten out of that cold miserable place (his words, not mine---no offense intended to those who live in and love North Dakota). Just a few weeks prior to that I heard two of my friends who are farmers talking about an acquaintance who farmed in another county and had an oil well producing 800 barrels per day. They were doing estimates of how many days it would take for that well to pay for a tractor---not just any tractor but the biggest and best. The conversation proceeded on about how long it would take for the well to pay for a new combine.

This all reminded me of how people will view things differently based on their perspective, experience, training and maybe genetic predisposition. What one saw as a ticket to get out, the other saw as a ticket to stay in. For that person working in the drilling industry, his job is very often what he DOES. For the person who has ties to the land, farming and ranching is what he IS.

Actually it is a little more complicated than that because drilling can "get in your blood too" as some say. I had been away from drilling rigs for several years and there was a well being drilled between our house and town. As we drove by, I was explaining some of the details of the operation to my wife and son. My wife said, "You miss it, don't you?" I answered that what I really missed was the pay check. Also, I missed the challenges of the job and I was curious about some of the newer technology but that I did not like the idea of being away from home for long periods of time.

It's not that the men who work the oilfields are not serious and dedicated to their jobs. They are there, regardless of the weather and working hard. The mindset is possibly affected by the sense of ownership. The person who questions why the farmer just spent all that money on a new tractor has a perfectly good explanation as to why he just bought a new four wheel drive pick-up with all the bells and whistles. He needs it to get to work. We each have our own perspective.

Maybe some psychiatrist will figure out our mindset someday. However, in my limited experience, I have never seen a cowboy who got dressed up as a roughneck and played oilfield on his days off.

LW8...Oil About Ranching...Water

A lady insisted that I say something about water and ended the statement with the age old question, "What are we going to do when we run out of water?" I have more questions than answers but maybe this will stimulate some discussion and hopefully somebody will find a solution. Maybe some high school student in a chemistry lab will not be limited by the thought of why it can't be done and will come up with an economical way to remove salt from water.

A substantial amount of fresh water is used in the drilling process. The initial drilling phase, or the surface hole, must be drilled with fresh water to prevent contamination of any and all fresh water zones that may be encountered. Each casing string that is set must be cemented in place and that takes more fresh water. The amount of fresh water used in the drilling phase is minimal compared to the amount of water required for the big frac jobs.

Although not an expert on fracking wells, a front row seat for the show has provided opportunity for observation. It is fascinating that somebody developed a process whereby water and chemicals can be injected into the specific shale zone and it will yield oil. Some of this technology is very new and it is reported that the process only works effectively with fresh water. Sources indidcate that there are labs working to find a process that will work effectively using brackish or brine water. One project had a team on site where some of the flow back water was being treated to be re-used on the next frac job. However, the details and success or failure of that project is not readily available. It was encouraging to know that somebody is working on it.

Not much information is readily available about current developments and companies are tight lipped about their research, understandably so. What we do know is that there are significant financial incentives for converting salt water to fresh water. At the present time, oil companies are paying to dispose of produced salt water that come out of the well with the oil and is then separated. Then they are paying for fresh water to use in the drilling and fracking. Economics is a major emphasis for a solution to this dilemma.

Hopefully, somebody has already found the solution and is in the advanced stages of the patent process. In answer to the question a "What will happen when we run out of water?", there have been three times that I've sold cattle due to dry weather and the fourth is rapidly approaching. The answer is the same in just about any busines: When you're out of water, it's over.

LW9...Oil About Ranching   Fracking

In order for oil to be produced from a formation there must be porosity and permeability. The pores that contain the oil must be connected by some sort of opening so that the oil can flow to the wellbore where it is pumped to the surface. Visualize a section of the bubble wrap packing material with the bubbles each containing oil with several hundred layers stacked together. Instead of the plastic bubble wrap, think about it as being sandstone or shale and then compressed together with more than two thousand pounds pressure per square inch, based on a depth of 5,000'.

When the zone is drilled, there may be some evidence of oil but it may not flow freely into the wellbore. For the oil or gas to flow through the formation, the walls of the "bubbles" containing the oil must be broken. Hydraulic fracturing has proven to be an effective method for breaking the structure so that the oil trapped and isolated in the "bubbles" can flow. First the zone must be isolated so that the pressure will go to the desired location. Then a mixture of water and chemicals that form a substance similar to gelatin are combined with a specified amount of sand and pumped into the formation.

While a normal pressure gradient may be approximately 2,000 psi, the pressure to fracture the formation may be more than three times that amount. When the formation is fractured, or fracked, the gel and sand mixture are pumped into the formation. The purpose for the gel is to be the element for putting the pressure on the formation. The sand is for the purpose of wedging into the cracks and then propping the cracks open so that the oil may flow through. The sand must be of uniform size so that each grain has an equal chance of staying in the desired location.

When the fracture begins, it is important that a large quantity of material be pumped down hole as quickly as possible. Seeing a dozen pump trucks connected and pumping together utilizing a combined sum of nine-thousand horsepower is quite a sight to see. The teamwork that is required and the logistics of getting everybody and everything in the right place at the right time is a serious challenge.

On some of the larger frac jobs with more than thirty stages, the process may require from four to seven days with the job running twenty four hours per day. When something breaks down or plugs up and the frac job is disrupted, the delay starts a ripple effect because there are trucks on the road brininging material to meet the pre-determined schedule. The schedule must be planned for everything to work with perfection but the contingency plan must be ready to deal with problems.

After one stage is fracked, it is isolated with a plug, and tools are run in to perforate for the next stage to be pumped. After all of the stages are completed on the frac job, the frac equipment is moved out and a coil tubing or well service rig is brought in to drill out the plugs used between each stage.

Sometimes with all of the traffic going in and out from a well site, it must appear to be total chaos but there is "method in the madness" and varied technical experts are performing their duties with precision. It's not unlike a branding crew where everybody knows what they are to do and when to do it. As I watch the teamwork of the crews working together I realize that their participation in a school band, athletic team or some FFA or 4H competition may have been a very important part of their education. They know that each team member has an important duty and responsibility.

LW10...Oil About Ranching...Learning Differently

There are no signs on the gas pump saying "Thank A Roughneck" and nothing like the NFR, Western Heritage Classic or Roping Fiesta to celebrate the heritage and skill. Most people working directly in the oilfield did not have the dreams and goal for doing what they are now doing. The oilfield has many success stories for those who worked hard when they received a second chance.

In meeting many of the workers in the oilfield, it can be discovered that a large number did not like school and did not do well in school. It has become very obvious that some learn quickly when it is on-the-job training where they can learn through their hands on experience. They know how to disassemble, move and re-assemble a drilling rig and put all the components together, yet some intellectual type (possibly earning less than half as much) who can't change a flat tire on their car, may comment that the rig workers "aren't very smart".

When observed closely, it is amazing how smart that some of the roughnecks prove themselves to be by learning how all of the varied equipment functions and what it takes to keep it running.

My wife is a school teacher and for several years has worked with students who have difficulty in learning to read. The education system has this set up as a "confidential" program, so I do not know the students she is teaching until some parent comes to me and tells how much they appreciate her efforts and success in helping their child learn to read.

As she has told me some of the fundamentals regarding students with whom she works, she would talk about how smart they are and how they have the ability to learn but they may learn differently. If the success stories of students with whom she works were publicized then her accomplishments, and those of other teachers like her, would be recognized as being more significant than an athletic coach winning a state championship. For her it is not about the accolades, it's about the children and about helping them to develop.

The evidence is readily apparent in the oilfield that some who did not do well in school can succeed in a very demanding profession. When I see some of the symptoms of reading difficulties which my wife has described, I think about the difference that might have been if that person could have had a teacher like her to help them.

Much of the traditional "hard labor jobs" in the drilling industry are becoming more technically oriented. With all of the computerized controls on equipment, all of the rig hands have had to step up to meet the new challenges. It parallels what I've seen happening with technology in farming and ranching. Some of these kids who grew up playing video games now quickly learn how to run the joy stick control on the modern drilling rigs. However, they must be able to read and follow instructions. I'm reminded that if we can read, we need to thank a teacher.

LWil...Oil About Ranching...Environmentalists

Most ranchers and farmers cringe when they hear the word "environmentalist". The irony of this term and the reality is that ranchers and farmers are and have been among the leaders regarding stewardship of the environment. Apparently, there are many in the environmentalist movement who would immediately shut down most production agriculture along with eliminating drilling for oil and gas with no consideration of how it would effect their food supply and lifestyle.

One of the scary things about environmentalists is that they seem to have too much time available to devote to whatever "cause" in which they choose to be involved. Their time does not seem to have the type of limitations of those who are working sixty hours a week to produce food, fuel and fiber. It seems that they have much more time to be vocal and promote their ideas. It's also much easier to point blame than to design solutions.

Regardless of our profession and what we produce, we are impacted by environmentalists. I'm frustrated by the environmentalists who simply perceive a problem as if they have made an initial discovery and it is imperative that something be done immediately. There is nothing like watching someone who thinks that they have just invented the wheel. They are usually unaware that ranchers, farmers and oil producers may have been making progress on that very issue for several decades. Communication and education is very important.

It appears that evolution has not helped the environmentalists very much as I have seen very little improvement in their development over the past forty years. The same credibility issues exist with most of them who continue to be dependent on someone else to provide their food, housing and transportation. The credibility of environmentalists usually diminishes rapidly when their lifestyle and transportation are examined. One who lives in an adobe house, harvests rain water, raises a garden, milks a goat and co-exists with free range chickens and does not use motorized transportation is one who might be literally walking the walk and have enough credibility to be a concerned and pro-active environmentalist.

One of my earliest encounters with so-called environmentalists occurred around 1980 when I worked for Big Oil and happened to be in the beautiful city of Ft. Collins, Colorado and had an occasion to meet some young ladies who were students at Colorado State. Upon learning that I worked for Big Oil, they decided that I was to blame for all of the pollution, destruction, waste and desecration that had ever occurred. Then and now, the enviros play the blame game and want to force you to play defense.

Instead of arguing with them, I decided that there should be some mutual idea on which we could agree. Rather than try to defend my position, I submitted the idea that it was all about supply and demand and that if they would simply stop buying oil & gas then the problem would be solved. To which they responded, "If everybody stops buying gas and goes back to riding horses for transportation, then you wouldn't have a JOB!" The voice inflection was a combination of derisive, condescending, somewhat threatening and with a hint of class distinction coming from someone who had probably never had a job and probably had no marketable skills for a job.

I responded that I would be very happy about the prospects of going back to horse transportation and that I definitely would have a job because I would open a livery stable and not miss a day's work.

Now I have a wagon and team so am more ready than ever to look into the Livery Stable business. I wonder how many forms, environmental studies, zoning laws, OSHA reviews and EPA regulations would be involved? Meanwhile, I better get out and drill another well.

LW12...Oil About Ranching...Horizontal Drilling

Horizontal drilling is a subject that frequently brings up some questions. Yes, we really do drill straight down, then make a gentle angle curve with the wellbore and then drill horizontally through the desired section. The drill pipe actually does curve and later the casing is set through the curve. For those of us who learned about metal fatigue by bending and flexing baling wire until it broke, it is difficult to believe that the pipe can be curved ninety degrees without failure. Sometimes I actually stand on drill site and have difficulty believing that we are actually bending the pipe ninety degrees and drilling.

The well is drilled vertically for a few thousand feet then a downhole hydraulic motor, which is a motor built inside of pipe, is picked up and used to drill the curve and horizontal section. It is powered by the rig pumps that pump the fluid that turns the pump, cleans the ground up cuttings away from the drill bit and pumps these cuttings to the surface. The drill pipe can also be rotated by the rig power. The driller can use either system to rotate the drill pipe or use in combination which provides faster drilling because of the combined RPM's delivered to the bit.

The downhole motor will either be adjustable or have a "bent sub" which is machined to have an angle that may be 2 degrees. Located above the motor is a "Measured While Drilling" (MWD) tool that is coordinated with the bit so that the drillers can look at instruments on surface and see which way the bit is facing. The 2 degree angle establishes the direction of the bit.

With all of the instrumentation it seems like it should be a simple process to set the direction of the bit face. The inconsistent variable in the process is that when the drill pipe is turned at surface the amount of turn that is transferred to the bit will not be exact due to torque and friction. This is when the skill of the drillers is very important because the instruments can do only so much and the drillers have to make the adjustments to compensate for the variables.

When the bit is set in the desired direction, the drillpipe is not rotated. Only the hydraulic motor is used to turn the bit. The idea is for the bit to sort of cut a groove to start the turn and the drill pipe will provide weight for the bit and "slide" down hole rather than rotate. Drilling is rotating the pipe and sliding is without rotation. Typically there will be 15-20 feet of sliding and then the pipe will be put in rotation and drill 15-30 feet to be sure that the curve is being made on a very gentle and consistent rate.

Starting with the 2 degree bend, sliding and rotating, the well bore is gently turned 90 degrees in a span of about six-hundred feet. Look at the curve on a rail line spur and see how much that it may curve in the length of two football fields. Then the well bore is laid out horizontally to drill through the desired section. All through the curve and horizontal section the angle and direction are continually monitored and adjustments are being made to keep the hole straight so that the production casing (pipe) can be put in without trouble. Every kink and wobble presents a problem by creating friction. Many readers of this column have had a post hole auger stuck in a hole only three feet deep. The greater distance creates more opportunity for problems.

There are several advantages to drilling horizontally. It may expose more production formation area than eight wells drilled in a row. Only one drill site and pit area must be constructed.   One limiting factor for horizontal drilling is that the formation strata must be consistent and of adequate dimensions so that the driller can have a reasonable target to maintain.   A straight target with a ten foot variance requires a minimum thickness of twenty feet plus some contingency is needed beyond that.   If the zones are thin and irregular, then horizontal drilling is not an option.   While the cost of drilling one horizontal well with an eight well equivalent spacing may not be as much as drilling eight vertical wells it is a big investment.   The downside is that if there is a failure and the well is lost it is equivalent to losing several wells.   Another requirement is that the lease must have enough acreage to have the distance to drill the desired horizontal section.

Almost every discussion about horizontal drilling has somebody asking the question about the possibility of crossing lease lines.   This is one of those situations where the integrity of the operator and several contractors is the main thing that prevents encroachment.   It's not much different from the question about one rancher rounding up a few of his neighbors calves and taking them to the auction.   The law and the penalties may be important but it is the individual integrity that primarily prevents the problem.   There is usually a no-go limit that is set by the operator to provide some margin of safety about getting too near the lease line.

When looking at all of the technology used in drilling horizontally, we never hear anybody say "It's not rocket science" because much of the technology has come from the aerospace industry and exploration.

Horizontal drilling is somewhat like instrument flying. It takes a lot of trust in those instruments to get to the destination.

LW 17...Oil About Ranching...Oil Production in Texas

Oil production has risen significantly in Texas during the past two years. Statistics posted by the Texas Railroad Commission (the regulatory agency for oil & gas in Texas) show that Texas averaged about 30 million barrels per month for the years 2007-2010. In 2011 there was 23 percent increase to 37 million barrels per month and in 2012 there was a 29% increase to 47 million barrels per month. The first four months of 2013 show an increase of 6% to slightly more than 50 million barrels per month.

For the 28 month period through April 2013, if those statistics and my calculator are correct, that is an additional ONE BILLION dollars of net raw product produced in Texas each month. This is the actual dollar increase of Texas product and does not include the multiplier effect of the number of jobs produced and additional goods and services to achieve this production and distribution.

This is having an effect on the ranching and farming industry. The good news is that most of these new jobs are going to people who are good customers for the rancher because they are more likely to eat a double patty burger instead of tofu and sprouts. The bad news is that many acres that were once in production agriculture are now used for oil field locations and roads.

No doubt that somebody, somewhere, is crunching these numbers but I haven't seen much reporting on the direct effect that these added dollars are having on our economy. Like most people, my perspective is usually about as narrow as the space between my horses ears. The tunnel vision tendency causes me to see only that which has a direct and immediate effect on me. Usually, there are many things happening all around us that we don't pay much attention until we suddenly realize that the landscape has changed.

The question often comes up about how the oil boom is having an impact on individuals and communities. Last week a man who lives in Abilene told me that just the rumors of the big Cline Shale boom that is "coming soon" has already caused an increase in rent and property values. He went on to say that it will probably affect everything and that everyone will be affected in one way or another. Most people who live in "boom towns" will probably agree with him.

Those of us who participated in the oil boom of the early 1980's thought that we had participated in the biggest oil boom that would ever occur. Plus we were told by the "experts" in the following years that the Permian Basin was depleted and in a decline and that it was just all downhill.   New technology changed everything. The construction activity in the Midland-Odessa and surrounding area far exceeds anything that we saw in the 80's.   There is some new construction and renovations in Sterling City.   Several equipment yards are under construction along Interstate 20 between Sweetwater and Midland.

One rancher said that his monthly royalty checks are so big that they are "scary". He didn't define why they were "scary" but based on the oil production that he mentioned, the checks could well be in excess of the FDIC coverage limits at the bank. This is a problem with which this writer has absolutely no experience.

A realtor said, "Business is good. Real good". He went on to say that not all of the customers are directly related to oil but that the oil business has improved the economy and the attitude in Texas and that interest is real estate has improved.

You can check the production and other statistics at the TRRC website: http://www.rrc.state.tx.us/   As of July 19 they reported 836 land rigs working in Texas which is about 47 percent of all the active rigs in the U.S. The surge in drilling activity and oil production is probably going to affect all of us in one way or another, even for those who are not involved in oil or ranching in boom areas.

LW18...Oil About Ranching...Surface Owner/No Royalty

A reader, who I know but had not heard from for several years, called a few days ago with the following question: "How does a surface owner, who has no mineral/royalty interest in the underlying property, protect himself regarding damages and activity that may occur on the property?" My first response was to remind him that I am not an attorney so am unable to provide legal advice, (that and all other appropriate disclaimers apply). My suggestion was to get an oil and gas attorney for advice.

I agreed to include his question in an article in hopes that we could get some feedback from readers who have dealt with the situation where they owned or operated the surface but had no royalty/mineral ownership. It is my understanding that the mineral interest below the surface has precedence and that the mineral owner cannot be denied access. There is a possibility that a lease of the underlying property may be in effect before the landowner is notified of the intent to drill a well on the specified property. Damages are usually paid to the surface owner and the term "reasonable and customary" is one that I've heard used several times.

It is possible that the lease may have some specifics that provide some protection for the landowner such as no drilling locations or production facilities within a specified distance from a dwelling. If it is not specified in the lease, it will be something to be negotiated with a representative from the oil company who handles claims and right of way issues. Hopefully, this will all be resolved before any construction or drilling begins on the property. The company representative or consultant involved in drilling operations is probably NOT authorized to make any changes or authorize additional compensation regarding surface issues.

A few notes that may be beneficial to have your oil and gas attorney consider during negotiations. 1) Absolute distance limit regarding drilling in proximity to dwelling or other significant location. 2) Location of an entry way and whether a cattle guard and/or gate is to be used. Please pick the safest place with the best visibility if possible to reduce the hazard for people getting on and off the roadway. 3) Hunting leases that may be affected. In some cases the oil company may schedule around hunting season, may offer to buy-out the hunting lease, or the location may be such that there is little or no impact. 4) How will livestock grazing or farming be affected? Do the pits or possibly entire location need to be fenced? In my opinion, the livestock owner is going to be much happier if no livestock are in the pasture during drilling operations. Maybe the cost of fencing the pits could be accepted by the landowner for agreeing to have all livestock removed from the area during construction and drilling operations. This might be a good way to rest some pastures and get paid for it. 5) Be definite regarding who will handle negotiations and specify who will be receiving damages. 6) Specify in writing who is authorized to handle negotiations. Negotiating with a "committee" of several heirs with various evolving priorities is probably not going to be enjoyable for anyone involved.

Two leases in close proximity had significant differences: In both cases, there was a grazing lease in place. On one property the person with the grazing lease received payment for the surface damages and on the other ranch across the road, the damages were paid to the landowner. The person with the grazing lease who did not receive damage payments was very unhappy with the oil company but apparently did not want to confront the surface owner in fear that the surface owner might cancel his grazing lease. Just a reminder to make notes and cover ALL the pertinent details and be sure that they are written in the contract.

A Crockett County rancher, who is one of the most pleasant landowners where I have been involved in a drilling operation, recommended getting a "good" oil & gas attorney to be involved in the lease and contract negotiations.

LW19...Oil About Ranching...Reclamation

Reclaiming a drill site is serious business and landowners and oil companies do have assistance available. The Permian Basin Oil & Gas Stewardship Conference was held in Crane on August 13 with the primary subject being the restoration of drill site locations and pipe line right of way. This was sponsored by the Texas Agricultrultural Extension service and included a speaker from the Caesar Kleberg Wildlife Research Institute and the Texas Railroad Commission, among others.

Native grass seed was one topic that caught my interest. Research proved that native seeds provide the best long time cover and that it is important to use native seeds from the same area. Examples were shown that the seeds from the same plant variety but from a different region might not perform the same. Work is being done to help develop native seed sources in the areas where drilling and construction occur on a large scale.

One of the concerns presented is the timing for seed planting and that some contracts simply state the site must be seeded. Many people may choose the opportunity to get it done at the time that the area is being reclaimed because that is when the equipment and personnel are on site. The risk of postponing it is the risk of it not getting done. It was stated that "the best time for planting seeds is in the springtime just before a rain", which was received with unanimous agreement.

One ranch manager from the Snyder area stated that he had the small mesquite brush pushed back over the area after the pipeline was covered and that he believed that the brush provided protection with the shading and physical protection. I have seen grass with seed heads under small brush cover when the rest of the pasture has been grazed off prior to seeds being produced.

It was really good to hear about the work with native grass seeds and see that work is being done that is getting back to the basics instead of focusing on something new and exotic. Driving back from the meeting I got to thinking about how long that a grass seed may lay dormant and then sprout. I've heard estimates that seeds may last twenty or more years and then sprout when the timing is just right. When our normal dry weather pattern has been interrupted by some nice rain, plants may appear that haven't been seen for years. I went into a pasture when I got home and saw some native grass headed out. It looked like it had been planted just before a nice rain. We received 6 ½" of rain over a three day period in July. There was cloud cover and it was wet for the duration of the three days. Several people have commented that they had never seen anything like it in July in this area. It would be interesting to know how long those seeds have been laying around waiting for just the right moisture and temperature conditions.

The conference was a reminder that landowners do have resources to assist them with efforts to reclaim areas that have been disturbed. Some dirt contractors have experience in working with the Ag Extension Service and the NRCS, still known by many as the Soil Conservation Service. There is help available to landowners for planning reclamation and locating native seeds. We can use many of these (tax funded) resources at no additional cost.

It is difficult to remember to get all of the details in the contract for reclaiming an area. More than one person commented that they had been told what would be done to reclaim the area but it was not done as had been discussed. My question "Was it in writing, in the contract?" Another reminder, if it's not in writing, it doesn't count.

A speaker from the Texas Railroad Commission went over the laws regarding the requirements in the State of Texas regarding how long pits may remain open, de-watering, and reclaiming the site to original grade. Landowners do have a friend in the form of the TRRC. There are laws that protect the landowner. If anybody is interested, I'll tell them why I think that the Texas Railroad Commission is one of the best government agencies in existence.

LW20...OIL ABOUT RANCHING...WYOMING LEASE

A reader from Wyoming suggested that lease and right of way agreements should specify the dimensions for roads and locations. Some landowners do not want any traffic to get off of the road or location. This is another case where it is important to have it in writing so that each party may avoid some confusion as to just what is meant. In some cases the right of way may be sixty feet wide for the road but the oil company may only put caliche or gravel to cover an area that is twelve feet wide. To accommodate opposing traffic it is necessary for one vehicle to get off of the improved roadway. Just because they are off of the improved portion of the road may not mean that they are in violation of the agreement regarding how much road is being used.

Due to cost, most drilling locations are only improved with caliche or gravel to meet the minimum needs for heavy equipment. The location pad may be 200' X 300' but the defined location may allow a useable perimeter around the location. This was the case on one ranch where the owner was very particular on details and did not want trucks getting off of the location into the pasture. Fortunately, in that case it was detailed in the contract that the "location" was much larger than just the improved "pad".

Most of us probably rely too much on the hope that "common sense" will be used by each party involved. Usually, it is advantageous for roads to be on the high ground when possible. Some people want all roads to be straight or to be adjacent to fence lines where possible. It may be okay to destroy any and all of the mesquite and cedar but to not get close to any oak trees.

Hopefully, all parties will be in agreement that safety takes precedence. One hazardous situation existed on a ranch where they insisted that the old roadway could not be re-routed. The roadway crossed through a small drainage area with a cross fence going through at the lowest point and a cattle guard at that point. During wet weather, which may be rare but seems to occur at the busiest time, trucks could not get up the hillside on either side. Every time that a truck became stuck it totally blocked the roadway. If emergency vehicles had been needed by either the drilling company or the rancher, the emergency vehicle had no access. Having to pull the trucks with a dozer created a less than safe operation and added to the cost and frustration for all involved.

One drilling crew in the early 80's was glad to learn that having all the details in the location specifics worked in their favor. A surprise search for illegal substances occurred on a well site during a rig move. With so many trucks hauling equipment, the driller decided to park a little farther away from all the traffic. When his crew car was searched, an ice chest with beverages made from fermented grain was discovered in the trunk. The rules specified that these type beverages were "not allowed on location". It turned out that the car was not "on location" and therefore it was not subject to search. They got by on a technicality. If the rules had stated "on the property" it could have been different. Being very specific in what is written can work more than one way.

The Wyoming rancher told about a situation where the BLM was involved concerning the sage grouse. The access preferred by the rancher would have resulted in a road being 1/8 mile in length. The road approved by the BLM was 1 ½ miles in length. Part of the land that he ranches is state lease with federal owned minerals. It must be very challenging to participate in multi-party negotiations, especially where some of the participants have no skin in the game.

Big trucks and equipment require significant space to maneuver. To get an idea of how much space is needed for a roadway, go measure a county road, fence to fence and the improved portion. Both are probably wider than the average person will guess. Be sure there is enough space to keep it safe and be sure that it is in writing.

LW21...Oil About Ranching...Economics of Production

Oil prices are above $100 per barrel and the general assumption seems to be that the oil companies must be making a lot of money. These comments are often followed with the presumption that the oil business would just continue to expand. In discussing the continual growth with one farmer, the question was posed to him about expanding his operation and what he would do if he had the opportunity to lease a couple of sections of wheat farmland twenty miles away. This was seasoned with the tempting assumption that wheat prices would be fairly good and that wheat grazing would be profitable with cattle prices at current levels.

His response was that there was no guarantee that those prices were going to stay at current levels. This was followed by the comment that it would require additional equipment and that he didn't think that he'd be able to find somebody dependable to handle the labor and that distance would be even more added expense. He summed it up saying that he had all that he could handle and was not interested in expanding or taking on more risk.

Some oil companies may be in a similar situation because they have been going at a fast pace for some time. Dealing with office staff, field personnel and various contractors may, at some point, result in boom fatigue. They simply get tired and may need to simply re-group and re-load. Oil people can sometimes suffer from the affliction of using the false premise of historical comparisons that get some livestock operators into a position of thinking that they must be making a profit based on current high prices. For the outsider looking in at a stocker operator selling steers at a dollar and forty cents per pound, it seems reasonable to make the assumption that the steer business must be a lot better than it was when steers were selling for seventy cents. Sometimes it is dangerous to let ourselves believe that we are doing as well as what some people may imagine. It's better to take a reality check while on top instead of waiting for it to catch up when things bottom out.

Some of the horizontal wells may cost more than seven million dollars to drill and frac. Royalties and operating expenses come off the top, before there is any return on investment. Each well must make a significant quantity of oil for the well to break even. Many times, a drilling rig will spend more money per day than a producing well will make. At some point, with several wells drilled and producing the cash flow may exceed the drilling and operating costs. The operation may be technically "profitable" and yet have a cash flow that is below projections.

For a project to be economically viable, an oil company needs to get enough production for a quick payout. For instance a company may base a project on an eighteen month payout. This may sound like a quick return on investment, but there are no guarantees and the operating expenses may increase even when the production income decreases. Many wells have a rapid rate of decline in production in the first two or three years. With the risk that exists and unknown production costs that may occur, an eighteen month payout for a well is not as much "all profit" as it may appear to an outsider.

Missing production targets by a few percentage points can have a significant impact on cash flow. A company that has five rigs contracted may see that the production is missing the target and decide that in order to meet the cash flow obligations comfortably, they will reduce their drilling activity and release one or two rigs to cut down on expenses. There may be one rig in the group that seems to be the one that has the most difficulty and seems to create the most problems. The decision may be made to optimize the operation by eliminating what appears to be the major source of problems. Or it may simply be time to take a breather and slow down just a little and stop the continual expansion. Adjusting the pace into a comfort zone and taking care of what they have is more important than trying to continually get more.

Oil and steers have similar common denominators; when oil goes through the meter or steers go across the scales then all the forecasts and estimates meet with reality.

LW22...Oil About Ranching...What is Expected

A reader asked if I would write something about what is expected from the landowner and what is expected from the oil company. The list of possible expectations would be exponential, but some thought and preparation may help prevent unrealistic expectations.

A leasing agent for an oil company probably does several leases every month and his expectation may be that this is routine to him and he wants to complete it in the simplest manner that is mutually beneficial for both parties. For a person who handles leases and contracts on a daily basis, it's not complicated and he probably has a reasonable expectation that the property owner will be satisfied with the standard or typical lease agreement that the company may use.

The property owner may be at somewhat of a disadvantage because this lease may be the only one with which they have ever been involved; or it may be one of a very few. The comfort level may not be very high but the excitement level may be extremely high. The excitement of doing the deal may interfere with the ability to think through the details. The parties to the negotiation are probably not equal in their experience.

Generally, both parties have a somewhat mutual expectaion and objective, which is to discover, produce and market oil and gas. The negotiation is probably not adversarial with a win/lose scenario but a mutually beneficial agreement that is a win/win for both parties.

In any negotiation, it is good to know the priorities of each party. One way to communicate the expectations is to make a list and prioritize the items into categories A, B and C. If everything is an "A" priority, it may be treated as a "B" list due to lack of emphasis on what is most important. My personal "A" list begins with protecting livestock and keeping them off the highway. Not having any livestock in the pasture when construction and drilling are in progress eliminates potential problems. The landowner must know the schedule for starting construction so that all livestock can be removed from the pasture. In some areas, the property is not fenced and livestock are not an issue.

A "B" item may be the placement of pipelines and electrical lines. An oil company probably expects to go the most direct and least expensive route. Exceptions to this for the property owner may be due to proximity to a dwelling or livestock pens or water systems.

Keeping all traffic on the roadway and location is a "C" priority for some, because there is a reasonable expectation that wide loads may need more space, weather problems may result in detours, etc.

One thing that may be unexpected and sort of an unintended consequence is the effect of the presence of numerous strangers on the property for an extended time. People who live in towns or suburbs do not have the same understanding of privacy and or space as someone whose "yard" is measured by hundreds of acres. Those of us who live in the country and who get to enjoy lots of space are in the minority. Even though we may accept that "our space" is going to be invaded, until we've been through it, we probably don't expect as much traffic, noise and activity as may occur.

One manager of an oil company that is involved in the very active area north of Barnhart told me that he was concerned that the people involved with the ranch, which is large and historic, did not realize that the oil activity was about to change everything as they know it. The landscape will never be the same. He may have had a more realistic expectation of how this was going to affect the people living and working on that ranch.

Expectations may include assumptions. Delete all assumptions and put it in writing.

LW23...OIL ABOUT RANCHING...
CREATION...9—16—2013.

What to do with the question about whether the oil bearing formations were created or is the oil the result of the theory that it was derived from decaying animals that were covered over by some earthquake or something and compressed for millions and millions of years?

I am not a geologist but do have an interest in the various formations and the differences in the composition of various layers. It is interesting that we can drill through several hundred feet of very hard formation and then hit a strata that is softer and easier to drill and then hit a formation that is very hard and abrasive and destroys a drill bit in a short time.

It was always perplexing that geological formations are identified as being of a designated age. Somewhat like asking about the distance to a town and getting an answer stated in hours rather than miles. After the Mt. St. Helen's volcano there was a report that when the molten rock that flowed down a river cooled and cracked there was a crevice that showed layers that were similar to some of the layers visible in the Grand Canyon. Although it happened in one day, the article claimed that the layers appeared to be of different ages. Several years after the eruption, I was hoping to see these layers but was told that the river had covered it.

Rather than get into my beliefs (being creation, but I am a regular creationist and not a fundamentalist; the two being very similar with the exception that the fundamentalists seem to be mad about it). I don't know enough about the structure and composition to argue the point about the age of the formations, so I resolved to just accept the "geological aging" as a measurement tool. That's the "marker" that they use and it is an established reference point. There is also the theory that time accelerates and moves faster as time goes on. That feels like a real possibility.

Oilfield hands and cowboys share a similar scenario where the work can often be described as hours of boredom interrupted by moments of sheer terror. If you have experienced being half asleep on a colt that suddenly downed his head and jerked the reins out of your hand, you get the idea. During one of these long boring spells, I was thinking about an oil field that had produced one hundred million barrels of oil. With an approximate weight of two hundred and forty pounds per barrel, it would take a lot of animals, everything from alligators to zebras carrying plenty of tallow to make that much oil. How could that many animals be gathered up in the one area then covered in such a manner that they are all in one layer? The numbers are mind boggling and this is just one area and there are other oil fields that have produced more than ten times that amount.

Some have claimed that the decaying animals accumulated over millions of years and then were covered by layer after layer of sediment and rock. As carcasses deteriorate, most of what would be a fuel source breaks down into a gas and goes into the atmosphere instead of waiting millions of years to be covered. The number of animals that would be required is mind boggling. To have that many live animals in one place at one time to be covered by a tectonic shift would be a round up far exceeding the accomplishments of Charles Goodnight and Oliver Loving. Even Noah's gathering would be small in comparison.

During my first oil boom, I remember a discussion about some of the formations that were being described as "young" and that they would take a few million more years to develop into oil bearing formations. I've often wondered if some of these formations that are now being fracked are the same ones that they were talking about being young and needed a few million more years to develop. Sometimes, that other oil boom seems like it was a real long time ago.

LW24...OIL ABOUT RANCHING...MORE OIL PRODUCTION

Oil production in Texas for the first six months is 8% above the average for last year. The Railroad Commission reports estimated production for June at 61 million barrels. 2012 production was 533 million barrels which is a new high for the past sixteen years. Like many others, I get tangled up in the present and need to back up and take a look at the history. The statistics for the past seventy years shows that Texas oil production peaked in 1973 at 1.257 billion barrels.

From 1943 to 1994 the average yearly oil production in Texas exceeded the recent record set in 2012. Even though there has been a big surge in production in the past three years, we're still a long way from the historical high production. The good news is that more production at home can reduce the need for imports.

Many people outside of the oil and ranching industry have the misconception that oil wells are flowing several hundred barrels of oil per day and that every ranch has thousands of head of cattle. The average per well production in 2012 was just under 9 barrels per day and the average in 1973 at peak production was less than 22 barrels per day.

In both industries, the small operators are very important. As wells get older and production decreases, the number of miles driven and hours put in by the pumper probably remain constant. As the equipment ages the repair and maintenance cost is more likely to increase rather than decrease. An oil well can be a textbook case for diminishing returns.

Often a big oil company may sell an oil field where the production has declined. A small operator may be able to operate more efficiently for several reasons. One reason is due to how a major company may treat the investment and the depreciation. For some companies, the total amount invested in developing a lease may remain allocated to that lease and their equipment depreciation may be averaged company wide rather than tracked on a well by well basis. The averaging has several benefits but also some pitfalls.

Back when wool was a valuable commodity, the story of success was told of buying some sheep, selling the wool and covering all expenses, selling the old ewes and "getting all their money back", and then owning the lambs free and clear. From that point forward, it might be viewed as having zero investment in the stock.

An oil company may produce enough oil in a given field to recoup the original investment many times over. However, rather than designating it as now being "free and clear" they must still carry that original and accumulated investment on the books due to their established accounting practices. Even though it has "paid for itself" many times over, the return on investment is still a consideration. Also, big oil will allocate overhead expenses to all leases. The overhead expenses from the big offices and high salaries may mean that some small leases are not even breaking even on the cash flow because too much cash has to flow to the overhead.

From a cash flow, it might appear that the field should be profitable. What might look like fifty percent return based on actual operating cost may only be a five percent return on investment. At least one big oil company refuses to "write down" the investment amount due to economic impairment. This keeps their accounting "clean" and Wall Street seems to appreciate that this company shows a true return and not something that is sometimes "adjusted". The company may sell a producing lease at a loss based on return on investment and maybe recoup only ten percent of their investment based on their accounting process. Then they will write off the "loss" rather than write-down to adjust their investment.

The independent operator with lower overhead may purchase an old lease and enjoy a good cash flow. Similar to a ranching operation, it's not just what is done, but also how it is done that matters.

LW25...Oil About Ranching...Engineers & O-Rings

Many years ago and old pumper made the statement that engineers and O-rings were what ruined the oil field. The engineers were always coming up with something new and different and he never could find the right size O-ring. While it got a few laughs, the opposite is true. Innovative engineers have developed new technology to get us where we are today. One article claimed that more improvement was made in diesel engines from 1995-2005 than in the previous ninety years and that is was due to new technology including extremely high pressure fuel injection systems. Better O-rings, or something similar are required for the higher pressure.

The new technology in the oil field has just about been overwhelming. The learning curve has been compared to getting a drink from a fire hydrant instead of a water fountain. While the new technology and new developments are impressive, the current engineers have the benefit of technology, of history and the experience of a vast number of engineers that have helped them along the way.

The oil field equipment business began fairly early in the Industrial Age. Much of the equipment today is of the basic design that was started in the early days. The tapered thread design on drill pipe is a good example. It is designed to support a tremendous amount of weight and can be screwed together and unscrewed many times with minimal wear or damage. There are several slight variations of the basic design but it's a very coarse thread that is virtually impossible to cross thread when making connections.

The hoisting mechanism, or draw works, is very similar to some equipment that was considered to be "old" when I first saw it over thirty years ago. The drilling line, or cable, looks just like it did the first time I went on a drilling rig but I'm sure that there have been improvements in the metallurgy and manufacturing process. A small number of engineers got things started with some good ideas and designs that are still in use today. It's like what some cowboys say about the mohair girth and Navajo saddle blanket and how "they got it right the first time".

The "iron roughneck" is an engineering marvel. This is used to make connections, that is screw the pipe together. Most of the iron roughnecks are not true robots and do not totally replace the human roughneck. A human is still needed to position, operate and maintain the equipment which uses more power to do the job more efficiently. The advances in hydraulics (by engineers and o-rings) have made the process of tripping pipe much safer. Throwing the chain and using a spinning cathead have been outlawed by many companies.

Hydraulic pipe handling equipment provides a much safer working environment. Some of the early models had a complex mechanical system powered by hydraulics and were prone to failure because of too many moving parts. The best one appears to be the simplest design. It has an angled groove in the cat walk and ramp and there is a chain driven mechanism that operates under the catwalk that powers the "rabbit" that runs in the groove and hooks the pipe and pushes it up the the V-door ramp. It's great when it works properly but it is high maintenance. The roughnecks today have to develop a high degree of technical skills to maintain modern equipment.

    Not all technology is an improvement. We were putting together a brand new rig near Hearne, Texas a few years ago and the blow out preventer control system for this new rig had been computerized. Not only did it have a computer to operate the system, it had another computer to run that computer. I know that sounds unbelievable because I didn't believe it either until the installation and testing. This over computerized control system was another case so someone trying to "fix" something that was not broken.

    We finally just pulled it off to the side of location and replaced it with the old style hydraulic/mechanical system with the manual control levers. In the situation of an emergency shut-in on the well, nobody wants a computer blocking the pathway. The only re-boot anybody wants to do during a well control emergency is pull off the steel toed boots and put on the track shoes.

LW26...OIL ABOUT RANCHING...ROYALTY TAXES

Some fortunate people with new wells drilled on their property will soon learn about paying county taxes on property where they have royalty income. If you are confused by this tax you are not alone. When I questioned one county appraisal district about the amount of taxes, I was told that it really shouldn't matter to me since I was just lucky and really didn't do anything to earn that income. How are you going to argue with being lucky and therefore paying taxes on being lucky? It wasn't a large amount and I thought that there was probably nothing that I could do that would make a difference.

A recent article in a big city newspaper related how the oil boom is helping the economy in many ways and included a statement that a percentage of the proceeds from oil and gas sales go into the tax fund of the county where the production occurs. While the article was providing information about how the oil boom was boosting the economy and not providing specific tax information, it may have left the impression that there is a set percentage of the royalty payment for county taxes.

Serving on the County Appraisal Review Board a couple of years ago provided an opportunity for me to learn a little about how the tax system functions. While being educational, that board is very limited and has no authority on the interpretation of the law and their only function is to listen to protests from taxpayers and then render a decision as to whether that taxpayer is being taxed on the same basis and rate as other taxpayers with like kind property. A few discrepancies were corrected and a few complaints were heard from people with no basis other than complaining that taxes are too high.

Taxes on oil and gas royalties are based on the appraised value of the producing property and not on a percentage of the oil and gas that is produced. It was explained that Texas is so opposed to a state income tax that instead of paying taxes on the "production income" that taxes are to be paid based on the valuation of the producing property. In this county, the local board does not do the appraisal on oil and gas properties. That is contracted out to an engineering firm. An individual with that firm explained that they based the value starting with the January production. That is compared to the previous January and calculations were made based on the typical decline of wells in that field. Not only does the predicted long term production of the property enter into the equation, they also come up with an estimated price of oil for the year.

My thoughts were that as a taxpayer, I am paying for somebody to make a scientifically well adjusted guess about how much oil a well may produce over a long period of time and what the average price of oil will be for the year. It appears to me that it would be much more accurate to apply a sales tax to the oil and gas at the wellhead and take the guesswork out of it.

One scenario that I witnessed that could have a significant impact on the taxes using the current method involved a well where a new zone was perforated with tremendous results. The well went from producing about 6 barrels per day to 140 barrels per day. Apparently, the zone was one of those unexplained over pressured zones and it had great production, but it lasted for only a short period of time. Given that this happened in early January, there was a significant surge in production for that month, which just happens to be the basis month for the valuation. In February it tapered off with a sharp decline over the next several months. This well did not fit into the set parameters and the surge in January production skewed the numbers. The owner was too busy to run all the numbers, do the research and file a protest.

A double whammy could occur with a surge in January production that is combined with a huge miss on the oil price prediction. If the guesstimation is off by 10X and the price falls by 60% (remember '08) there is a mathematical possibility that the tax paying royalty owner may develop a new understanding of diminishing returns.

Hopefully, this will remind ranchers who are getting royalty income for the first time to be vigilant and scrutinize the numbers. Do your own research and use your own calculator. Be sure and set aside at least one or more of those royalty checks for paying the county tax.

LW27...OIL ABOUT RANCHING...PRICE CONTROLS

All of the current buzz about the increased oil production in Texas could easily lead someone to believe (incorrectly) that we are experiencing the highest level of oil production that ever occurred. This pushed me to do a little research on the history of production and discover that we are now producing only about half what was being produced at the highest point.

It was intriguing to me that oil production in Texas hit a high point in 1973 (that being the same year that my knowledge level peaked as I graduated from college with a degree in agriculture economics). I was tuned in to the cattle business and worked a while for a feed company. The cattle wreck of '73-74 is reference point that still comes up in conversation and is a major reference point for many of us. Many of us believe that one of the contributing factors to that wreck was the implementation of price controls on the retail price of beef.

One of the lines coming out of Washington was that price controls wouldn't have any impact on ranchers because the controls only applied to the retail level. Of course, that statement was proved wrong in a very short time. In researching the price controls that were put in place in 1973 I was surprised to find that this was not the first time that price controls had been used on beef. President Truman did something similar in 1951. (learn from history?)

Even for some who lived the history in '73, we may not have seen as many pieces of the puzzle as we thought. My college time was during the cattle feed yard construction boom and shortly thereafter fat cattle hit an all time high, followed by a disastrous market crash. History shows that the country was in a "recession" in '73. It took decades for me to understand that the recession was the reason that the financial institution where I was expecting to go to work after graduation, reduced their new hire trainees from ten to five. Three days before graduation, the letter simply said that I was not one of the five. No explanation about the recession, I took it personally.

Back then, I paid no attention to the price of oil and was unaware that the price of oil was controlled by government mandates. The average price of oil had been between $2.50-3.50 per barrel from 1948-1971. President Nixon instituted price controls on retail beef. As the economy grew and demand increased, the crisis in the Mid-East saw oil prices surge to $12 per barrel in '74. At the same time that some over fed cattle were losing record amounts and we waited in lines at gas stations to purchase a maximum of ten gallons at a time. It was a real opportunity to get an education in real time about the adverse impact and (un?)intended consequences of government attempting to control prices. An interesting reference point was that in 1970 the average price of gasoline was thirty six cents per gallon and milk was $1.15 per gallon. Along with trying to pacify voters via their appetites by controlling the retail price of beef, the government also attempted to control the price of oil.

In retrospect, one of the most unbelievable parts of the price control on oil was that there was a two tiered pricing system. There was a set price for "old oil" and another price for "new oil". Due to the need for oil, the government was encouraging drilling but most new wells were uneconomical at the regulated price for old oil, so a price was allowed for oil that came from new producing wells.

Much of my understanding of economics came from wool and mohair production and the old government controlled incentive program. So, it was not a surprise that oil prices were under government control. However, the two-tiered oil price system was a strange thing to encounter when I went to work for big oil in 1978. Oil from old wells was restricted to $3 or $4 per barrel and new oil was about $10. Who could miss the possibility of the temptation to put some of the old oil in tanks with the new oil and sell it for three times as much? We were under very strict orders to monitor and control the handling of new and old oil and keep it separate. The company incurred a significant cost to keep the production separate. All companies may not have followed that strict procedure, but the biggest one was very clear that we were to obey the rules.

Again, my perspective is about as broad as the view between my horse's ears, but neither selective memory or limited research provides an incentive for government price controls. Something is ringing in my ears about learning from history or having to repeat it.

LW28...Oil About Ranching...Hunting Season Warning

Hunting season approaches with all of the usual excitement and expectations but some hunters may find that their favorite ranch has been re-decorated with imposing roads and oilfield equipment and traffic. All hunters need to be warned about the dangers involving the oilfield equipment.

One reader told about how he used the tank battery walkway as a shooting stand for hunting coyotes many years ago. He said it never crossed his mind that shooting his gun could be an ignition source to set off any gas vapors that might be present. The elevated walkway with such a good vantage point was probably more than just a temptation, it was more like it was put there just for his convenience. He was oblivious to any danger even though he grew up out in the country where common sense is valued more than prestigious degrees. Like he said, it's a miracle any of us survived.

Another temptation is the ladder on the pumping unit that is used for greasing the saddle bearing. Most pumping units are electric powered and are operated by an automatic timer. This means that they may start at any time with NO warning. There are many horror stories about oil field fatalities involving pumping units and someone being hit by the heavy counter weights that rotate. Most of the fatalities involve someone who was working on the unit and knew what they were doing but made one mistake. The potential hazard is so great that something more than just a warning is needed.

It probably wouldn't hurt to put it in writing as a memo or addendum to the hunting lease agreement that all of the oilfield equipment and facilities are "off limits" to hunters. Specify that the oil company has a lease agreement and that any encroachment on the property of the oil company can be considered as trespassing. Every hunter should probably be required to have a subscription to Livestock Weekly just so they could read this warning. There is no way to overstate the unseen hazards involving oilfield equipment that appears to be idle and out of service.

Pipelines can also be a hazard and vehicles should cross only at designated crossings. Poly lines are in use on many leases and may be used for everything from fresh water to natural gas. Hunters need to be aware of the pipelines. The right of way of a pipeline is often a ranch road that provides an opportunity for varmint hunting. Extreme caution is recommended. Hunters need to understand about watching for leaks or spills and report anything that appears to be out or order.

These warnings come from personal experiences, having tied my pony to the stairway and climbing up on the tank battery walkway to see if I could see where the sheep were located. At that time my age was measured in single digits. My curiosity made it necessary to open the hatches to see if there was oil in the tanks. I had probably been told to not climb on the stairway at the tank battery. Sometimes little boys don't process info. Fortunately, there was no poison gas and there was no static electricity to set off a spark.

The priority is to be sure that everybody survives. Then answer the questions about how the oilfield may affect the hunting. Wildlife will probably adjust to the routine maintenance level of oilfield activity but the heavy twenty-four hour traffic during the drilling phase may play havoc with the wildlife. Having witnessed a hunting lease fiasco with a bunch of unhappy hunters who didn't get any game and also did not get the peace and tranquility of prior years at that same location, there is a high probability that a surge in activity will have some short term negative effects.

Hopefully, this is something that the rancher has discussed with the hunters prior to their arrival. The best case scenario is that the hunting lease was considered in the oil and gas lease and/or part of the damages agreement. One goal of a hunting lease is to escape confusion and conflict and enjoy the outdoors. A safe hunting trip is a success.

LW29...OIL ABOUT RANCHING...WYOMING... PRIVATE PROPERTY

Working in different states really opened my eyes and caused me to have a broader and much better perspective about doing things differently in various regions. Many experiences near Big Piney, Wyoming are frozen into my memory. The standard joke of many residents of that area told about how they were looking forward to summer and that they hoped it came on a week end next year. A couple of years experience taught me that there was truth in that humor. Growing up near the center of Texas, the term "summer jacket" was unfamiliar.

In the early 80's some prolific gas wells were discovered in the area west and southwest of Big Piney. In the early fall of 1983 we began drilling a wildcat well called Fogarty Creek which established the final corner defining the field. The company's rig count for that area went from about three that year to ten the next year. The plans were to develop that field and build one of the largest gas plants in the nation.

The LaBarge project, as it was called, was very different to what I had witnessed in Midland, Texas and Elk City, Oklahoma. The local population was not large enough to provide the workforce required for the drilling of the wells and construction of huge pipelines and a massive gas plant. This was the beginning of my education about the differences between public lands and private property. My earlier knowledge of public lands was limited to city parks, public roads the space around public lakes.

My experience had been in areas where landowners received damage payments for locations and right of way easements along with royalty for oil and gas that was produced. Environmental impact and societal impact were relatively new terms. With the exception of a few businesses, most of the residents seemed to have negative feelings about the sudden boom. Looking at it through the eyes that had recently witnessed the 80's bust in the Permian Basin in Texas and the Anadarko Basin in Oklahoma where so many drilling rigs were stacked, my thoughts were about how much those areas would have appreciated a similar level of activity.

Soon, it became apparent that the surge of activity was going to be mostly negative for the residents. Since most of the damage and royalty payments were on government owned land, it created about as much excitement as they would be if they were being taxed at a rate of 100%. For most, it seemed that the added traffic and activity would be all negative.

During a conversation about hunting, a resident of Big Piney told me that he didn't think that it was right that Texans had all that private land where they didn't allow the public to hunt. He believed that everyone should be allowed to hunt on private land, same as public land and that access to it should not be denied. I was not arguing with him but listening to a foreign concept. Until that time, private property was something that I had taken for granted and never really thought about. This conversation was a catalyst for much thinking and study on private property rights and the impact that it has on our lives.

In the same conversation, he stated that he believed that they should not allow workers who lived out of state to hunt in Wyoming since they were just there working and didn't live there. He believed that only the people who lived in that area should be allowed to hunt on the federal land in that area. He did not realize that every U.S. citizen had as much right to federal land as anybody else. He saw no contradiction in his view that there should be unrestricted access on privately owned land far away but that he wanted restrictions on the access to "his" government owned land.

In a short time, it became obvious that some bureaucrat could devise more than one way to skin a tiger. Somewhere within the government lease agreements or the environment impact study, there was a clause that if any employee on the project was convicted of any fish and game violation, that the employee would be terminated and not allowed to work on that project. There were some unmarked homesteads on some of the federal land and some of the streams crossed through some privately owned surface with no markings. It was the fisherman's responsibility to know exactly where these were located and to avoid trespassing. The possibility of making an honest mistake of unintentional trespassing or bagging a wrong specie of fish was too great a risk and one for which most of us did not want to jeopardize our jobs. With all the work that we had to do, there was not much if any time for hunting and fishing. Nobody mentioned that "our rights were being violated".

We were not told that we couldn't hunt or fish but they changed the risk/reward scenario and increased the level of difficulty to the extent of decreasing the desire. Since then, I've thought a lot about private property and private property rights.

LW30...OIL ABOUT RANCHING...% OF SUCCESS

What percentage rate is considered successful? We hope for a 100% calf crop but do we really expect it? Is there a banker who will loan money with that being the basis for projected cash flow? Is 98% a more reasonable expectation and something that we would be willing to accept? These questions came to mind after I received a call from a big city reporter who was doing a report on the South Texas oil boom. He told me that he had no experience or knowledge in either ranching or the oil business. We had a very interesting conversation and his wide open unbiased questions were thought provoking.

He mentioned that he had gone to a livestock auction and visited with a rancher who told him that he was having trouble with all the traffic on the ranch and that "they" had left the gates and now he had bulls in the wrong pasture and that it was a real mess and summarized his feelings with the statement "they just don't care!"

That generalization is very frustrating and in most cases is not accurate. The problem with the gate being left open may well have been the result of a one or two percent failure rate. Of all the times that someone passes through a gate, it seems like it only has to be left open one time and some livestock will escape. In the case of the gate being left open, the problem was perhaps caused by a one percent failure rate. The flip side of this may have been a ninety-nine percent success rate, which would make the rancher's statement of "they don't care" to be only one-percent accurate. For the person who has a bull now in the wrong pasture, the ninety-nine percent success rate on those who properly closed the gate is irrelevant. The bull problem is now a priority.

It really doesn't matter if the gate was left open intentionally by someone who incorrectly thought it would be okay to leave it open because he would be back through in just a few minutes or if it was an unintentional mistake. It is highly probable that most oil field personnel who go through the gate have been working hard and putting in long hours and dealing with a multitude of conflicting priorities. After opening and closing so many gates, the motions can become somewhat automatic and not much thought is required. All it takes is a distraction by another "crisis" phone call coming in just after opening a gate. Suddenly the subconscious activity of opening and closing the gate is interrupted, the new urgency demands action because he just spilled the coffee in the seat while answering the cell phone and he is really mad because he was up all night and just got chewed out at the last rig for something for which he had absolutely no knowledge or involvement. Murphy's Law sometimes really kicks in.

Most of the oilfield workers abide by the rule of leaving gates like you found them. This rule is really simple and usually works until mass confusion occurs. Such as a string of traffic with each driver signaling the next one to close the gate and then somebody is coming from the opposite direction and somewhere in the traffic the signals get crossed up and the gate is left open. While the gate is left flopping in the breeze, a truck comes along and unknowingly catches the gate with the corner of the trailer, rips it off and drags it a quarter of a mile away. The next person is asked if he closed the gate and his response is "What gate, I didn't see any gate."

Most of us who raise livestock have back tracked several times to make sure that we turned a windmill on, turned the water off, opened the gate on the backside of the trap to let the stock out or opened the gate to the water lot so the stock would have water. Changing my wristwatch to my right arm used to be the reminder to turn off the water. Now, the cell phone alarm serves that purpose.

The odds are slim, maybe one or two percent, that a gate will be left open but there is a chance that it will happen and the risk is determined by the potential amount of damage that may occur and the time it will take to correct the situation. Handling livestock in an oilfield stretches the interpretation and application of compatibility. We'll keep trying for 100%. Every day there are some more new guys that need training. It's a challenge.

LW31...OIL ABOUT RANCHING...RESOURCE INFO

One reader sent a link to to www.recenter.tamu.edu and said to click on TIERRA GRANDE then go so the search box and type in "negotiating oil/gas lease". This lists several articles pertaining to leases. She went on to say that it had been a very helpful resource for her family and mentioned that she was currently participating in the "Annie Project" which is provided by Texas A&M Agri-Life Extension and is for women who own farm or ranch land. It was nice to learn that she had found a good resource that was beneficial to her. Maybe this information will be useful to others.

For many farmers and ranchers, a lease, such as a grazing lease or crop land lease, is an agreement between two people for a designated term and the lease is not transferable to another party. Typically, oil and gas leases may be sold or traded. This may leave it wide open to be sold to another company. One lease had a clause in it that in the event that the lease is sold by the lessee, then the lessor (in that case being the surface and mineral owner) had the option to purchase the oil and gas operations. The landowner might not have any interest in becoming an oil operator but this might provide some leverage or incentive for securing a more compatible operator in the case of an impending sale. It's an interesting idea and probably not anything new since the attorney who wrote the lease has been practicing for several decades.

The competitive nature of some people drives them to demand a lease that pays them more than what their neighbor received. There's nothing like being the winner at the coffee shop or bridge party, but that may not help the bottom line. A good thing to remember is that almost anybody with sufficient resources can buy an oil lease and a large number know how to drill a hole in the ground but it's a much smaller number who may have expertise in getting the maximum long term production. Like a horse race, the start is important and the hope is to look good coming out of the gate but it is the finish that really matters.

One really good oil lease deal that I witnessed in the 80's boom didn't produce a drop of oil. The lease payment was made and shortly thereafter the oil price declined and drilling activity practically ceased in the area. The lease term expired after two years and a rig never entered the property. That couple had been married over fifty years and used the lease money to purchase a much needed new car. They weren't big tourists but they did enjoy several short trips the following year which happened to be the last healthy year that they had together. When the lease expired without any drilling and there had been no more offers to lease the property, they were glad that they had accepted the offer that was presented to them. They were not concerned about a neighbor getting more or about money being left on the table.

Meanwhile, across the road, several neighbors have been tied up in a production "unit" for fifty or sixty years. That is an example that a lease can last a very long time. Second and third generations are now living with a lease agreement that was made a long time ago. It's just another reminder that an oil and gas lease has the potential to last a very long time.

Unitized production, or pooling, may occur when adjacent leases are combined to form a unit with each royalty owner having a percentage based on their property amount. Basically, it means just having a smaller piece of a much larger pie. There is the possibility that oil may only be found on one property and that owner ends up sharing with everyone else in the unit. Any individual can end up on either side of that issue. Over the years, there have been many complaints that I have heard about production "units" with the comment to "never get tied up in a unit". Many of us learned to never say never through a difficult process.

One advantage for unitized production is putting all the properties into one operating system for increased efficiency and is often done in order to enable enhanced production with water flood or CO2 injection to get more oil and gas from the formation. For enhanced recovery to be feasible, a significant portion of a reservoir will probably be needed. From an efficiency standpoint, it could be compared to fencing off each animal unit for grazing or combining with others to form a grazing association. At some point, putting it all together may be mutually beneficial.

Being aware of a couple of units that were held for many years with only one producing well for the entire unit is a reminder to consult with a good oil and gas attorney. For many royalty owners, enhanced production from unitized production has been a very good thing. It's probably a good idea to be cautious getting into a unit and have just as much knowledge as to how you will get out of the unit. As with a grazing association, everybody else might not want to be tied up by the whoever owns the last remaining longhorn steer.

LW32...Oil About Ranching...Oil Price, Rig Count

Oil price has dropped some over the past few weeks, down from $100 to about $95 per barrel during the last week of October. To most consumers, that still sounds high and many producers may be content with that price but they may keep a close watch on the slight decline. Most of the costs associated with drilling operations have been increasing. Just like any business, if the costs are going up and the revenue is going down, even slightly, it can have a significant impact on the cash flow. The good news is that drilling activity is still going strong.

The Oct. 13 rig count for the U.S. showed 1,738 land rigs working, which is down 1 from the previous week and down 88 from the previous year. The three most active basins and respective rig counts show that the Eagle Ford (South Tx.) 233 rigs, Permian (West Tx.) 463 rigs and Williston (North Dakota) 183 rigs. Texas had a total of 807 land rigs which is 46% of the drilling rigs at work in the U.S. Rig count is a mixed load of data and it's like sorting through a load of cattle containing steers, heifers, pairs, drys and bulls. One point of interest is that the horizontal count in Texas is 498 which is up by twenty from a year ago.

When we look at the possible impact that one horizontal well may be the equivalent of 6 or more vertical wells, the increase of twenty horizontal rigs in Texas may more than offset the decrease of eighty eight rigs overall in the nation. It's difficult to be definite because there are several more variables that apply. As a general rule, the horizontal wells employ more workers.

Usually there are two consultants or company men splitting day and night duty and a team of four who handle the horizontal tools and constantly monitor the direction and penetration. Along with the obvious technology on site, there are also various members of the behind the scenes support group for the technology and equipment.

After hearing some talk that drilling was going into a fourth quarter pull back because some companies have spent their drilling budget for the year, it's interesting to take an overview of the statistics and get a general idea regarding the activity. Although we are still looking at a mixed bag, the increased activity in horizontal drilling indicates more investment and more jobs.

The Texas Independent Producers and Royalty Owners Association (TIPRO) had an advertisement in the October issue of TEXAS MONTHLY stating that there are 388,000 oil and gas jobs in Texas and that the average oil and gas wage is more than double the rest of the workforce. There was no mention that many of the oil field workers put in many more hours, spend more time and money getting to the work location, spend a lot of time away from home and miss a lot of activities. Whenever some of my friends or acquaintances make an envious comment about how much oilfield workers are being paid, my suggestion to them is that steel toed boots aren't really very expensive and that they can get in on the action with a fairly small investment but to remember that it's a little bit like bull riding and that when they nod their head, somebody will open the gate and the view changes considerably.

TIPRO also noted that there are 570,000 Texas

Royalty owners. No details were provided about the average amount but my guess is that the 80/20 statistical rule might apply and that 20% of the royalty owners receive 80% of the payments. Regardless of how it is divided up, there are more individuals receiving royalty payments than the number who are working in the oil field. In some cases the numbers do overlap. If you believe in private property rights, this provides a good example to compare these numbers to government ownership of property where the subjects do not participate in the investment and ownership of property and royalties go to the government.

It was also stated that oil and gas companies pay 6 times more state and local taxes and royalties on a per job basis, $28,000 per employee, than the average private sector company. This indicates that not all multipliers are created equal. Every oil field job that we see is an indicator of much more activity than meets the eye. They report that the highest job multiplier in Texas is in the petrochemical manufacturing. Nearly 22 additional jobs are created for every oil and gas job.

The cliché "If you eat, you are involved in agriculture" is similar to the one about "the country that runs on oil can't afford to run short". We have many reasons to be thankful that production is UP.

LW33...OIL ABOUT RANCHING...ACRONYMS

When a cowboy says that he has been "nailing iron", just about anyone who has a moderate understanding of horse lingo will know that he has been putting shoes on a horse. A driller who says that he has it "turning to the right", is indicating that progress is being made according to plan. But it would be the exact opposite for a NASCAR driver who turns it to the right. Effective communication is a challenge within and across disciplines.

Recently, doing some contract work for a medium sized oil company, it came as quite a surprise that the company did not use abbreviations or acronyms on their reports. Every organization, business or profession has its own vocabulary, which tends to precipitate acronyms and abbreviations. A positive aspect of an acronym is to improve efficiency in communication and simplify record keeping and reports. Negative implications occur when the intent or application of an acronym or abbreviation is used to limit the amount of information available to anyone other than a select group. Plus the "in groups" are continually coming up with new buzz words in an attempt to sound enlightened.

Prior to computers and the insatiable information demands, the daily drilling reports were one page. These reports were called in to the main office about 6 AM where someone wrote down the information. It is no surprise that some of the common activities could be combined into something like CBUTOHLDIBS&Bit, PU new bit DHMSTRR,2DC's,RR TIH which is much simpler than writing out circulate bottoms up, trip out of hole, lay down integral blade stabilizer and bit then picked up new bit, down hole motor, steering tool, roller reamer, 2 drill collars, roller reamer and trip in hole.

The decision had been made, by the particular company, that the use of acronyms was causing more problems than solutions. By not using acronyms or abbreviations, it removed some of the guesswork. It is probable that the decision to spell things out was the result of some error in interpretation that resulted in a very expensive mistake. Having used many of the basic oilfield acronyms for more than three decades, it presented a challenge to remember to spell things out. The logical benefits of clarifying communications was evident, however the logic was soon abandoned in the area where daily activity is entered. A line of information might include something like Drill f/1,280' t/ 2,487', in that instance we were supposed to abbreviate from and to. (Always do it this way except when instructed otherwise??) Then tab over to the next block which stated, starting depth, enter 1,280; ending depth, enter 2,487. At the end of the report in the comments section we were instructed to use the appropriate template for the activity and summarize the days activity, where we again entered the data of drilling from, to, etc.

It seemed like it would be a good place for an Ace Reid cartoon showing a person saying "The redundancy seems to be getting repetitious", followed by his co-worker sighing, "You can say that again."

Sometimes, in the attempt to improve communications and reduce errors, the side effects of the cure is much worse than the disease. The logic of computer data entry is to enter each data segment only one time. If that is needed in multiple places, the computer program should perform the redundant steps.

The logical result of having to enter the same data three times just naturally increases the possibility of errors by three times.

Of course, this is nothing compared to what farmers and ranchers are subjected to by the NRCS which used to be the SCS which is next door to the FSA which use to be the ASCS. It was timely that just after I began working for the "no acronym" company that I received a newsletter from the local Farm Service Agency (or is that Authority?) that had the biggest conglomeration of acronyms ever seen. Having long suspected that there was some sort of interagency competition for the greatest number of acronyms, it's a good guess that this bunch qualified for the short go and is headed to the finals. When time allows, it will be nice to share with them the concept of the company that mostly abandoned acronyms. The info should be delivered ASAP.

If we didn't have a sense of humor, there's no way that we could survive the confusing communications. Recently, there have been several individuals who have commented about the value of effective communications in their businesses and organizations. One lady in a clerical position received an email from her boss that he had received a call from another department who had not received a report which she was supposed to have sent. She simply replied "I resent that." She had received notification of communication failure and had sent it again to the intended recipient. Not having a hyphen in "re-sent", her boss misinterpreted her message as "resentment" about his note to her. Some people do sweat the small stuff.

Most of the problems that I see within and between industries are communications related. One of my old habits is to give instructions to someone and then ask, "Do you understand?" Even the clueless respond with a high percentage of "Yes" answers. Gaps are discovered when they are asked to repeat the steps and plan of action. This is a reminder that those lease and right of way agreements may last a very long time and that the next generation may be confused by some terminology. At a recent cattle raisers organization meeting, we were briefed about an attempt by some group to delete the word "navigable" in a certain law. This could potentially have catastrophic impact on private property and water rights. Words mean things.

Be safe. The highways continue to be the most dangerous part of the oilfield.

LW34...Oil About Ranching...Thanksgiving

Thanksgiving 2012 was spent on a drilling rig near Barnhart, Tx. In 1980 my location was northwest of Craig, Colorado. Other than the fact that it sure beats looking for a job, being on a drilling rig on a special holiday is not where many people would choose to be. In both cases, and many in between, we did the best we could to have a feast of some sort and eat enough to compensate partially for being away from home. In 1980 the mud loggers (who were from New York) offered to cook the turkey for the crew and everybody on location that day. Every so often, a mud logger would comment that the turkey seemed to be shrinking as it cooked. Eventually they pulled out a Cornish game hen, to prove that the turkey really did shrink. We sure were glad when they pulled out a full sized turkey. Last year, at the rig near Barnhart, we combined efforts and prepared a feast. There's a real crowd on a big horizontal project. At least four states were represented.

Some people getting oil checks for the first time are especially thankful on this Thanksgiving. It's not just the size of the check but the incremental difference that it may provide. A man from Amarillo said that he had very small interest in some property and was smiling when he said that he gets a check for about a hundred dollars every three months. He said that he had consumed many good meals that were paid with those oil checks. It makes me wonder how many people have had the pleasure of taking in an oil check to make that final land payment, pay some college expenses, or simply make an anonymous gift to someone who they know really needs and deserves some help and encouragement.

A couple who I've known about all my life recently had a nice little well drilled on the farm where she was raised. Her husband has worked as an oilfield pumper for more than fifty years. They really have a special appreciation for that well. Sometime after the well began producing, the lady told me that they had just celebrated their sixty-third wedding anniversary. I made the suggestion that they should take a picnic lunch and go out to that well site to celebrate. She smiled and said, "We did that last night! What made you think of such a thing?" With a smile, my reply was "Been there. Done that." Having worked on wells in eight different states gave me a tremendous appreciation for a little oil production. For me, Psalms 23:5 is more than just a slogan. That appreciation for the oil production is similar to the reason that farmers and ranchers tend to be more thankful for the food that they consume; they know where it comes from and what was required to get it on the table.

When you give thanks for an oil check, here's a short list of those might also include. Geologist who picked the site, landman who secured the lease, attorney who protected your interest, engineers who developed the drilling program, regulatory agency who approved the drilling permit, construction crew who prepared the road and location, those who hauled the rig, tool pusher, driller, roughnecks, bit salesman, mud engineer, rental equipment providers, directional drillers & tool hands, casing crews, cementers, frac personnel, completion crews, tank builders, pumpers and a bunch of hotshot and truck drivers who haul everything from repair parts to hauling oil to the terminal and many other support personnel who all do their jobs with orchestrated precision (we hope). Also remember the on-site company man or consultant who gets blamed if anybody on the list (and anybody else who should be on the list) makes a mistake. And many more not covered in this list.

One of the advantages of getting older (and there's not as many of those as I had hoped) is having past experience to compare with the current activity. One of the nastiest dirties jobs around a drilling rig is that of the casing crew. As I was signing the invoice for a young man who was the crew chief on a casing crew I told him that I really appreciated their attitude and enthusiasm. He responded that he was making good money and driving a new truck and had every reason to have a good attitude. At the WRCA finals, a young man excitedly told me about his new job of driving a truck hauling frac sand. (If he can drive that truck as good as he played the mandolin, he's quite a driver.) He said that his longest wait time at a frac job was forty six hours and he was excited about the fact that he got paid for the entire waiting time. His excitement was contagious. And, no, I did not dampen his enthusiasm with a warning about how this boom too would end someday. It was too much fun, for a moment, to view this oil boom through some young eyes. He told me that due to the noise, he had difficulty sleeping while waiting on location for his turn to unload. I told him that he would get used to it and asked him to call me in six months to give me a report. By then, he probably won't be able to sleep without some roaring background noise.

We are having the best fall that we have had in years here in Runnels county. The recent rains produced a lot of grass. The cattle are fat and the prices are high. Yes, one of the best mineral supplements is a pump jack in the pasture. The horses are in good shape and there's a new litter of border collie puppies. Sometimes, it is really good to just stop and list the things for which I am thankful, especially for family and friends and hope that I can be better about thanks and about giving.

Many readers of this column lost a friend recently. In a tribute to him:

"Use the long rope to catch 'em and the short one to tie 'em. Take your time but hurry every chance you get." In memory of Max Horne, a Christian, family man who also shod horses for sixty years and roped a bunch of cattle. It was a blessing to have known him and an honor to call him a friend. Giving thanks for the memories.

LW35...OIL ABOUT RANCHING...DIESEL PRICES

Why is diesel so high? This is one of the most often asked questions. Although my work has been in exploration and production, it seems that I am held guilty by association for the high prices at the retail end of the business. Somewhat like the sheep shearer being blamed for the price of a wool coat at some fancy boutique.

A spot check of prices on Nov. 18, 2013, shows crude oil to be selling for $93.84 per barrel. At 42 gallons per barrel, crude oil is selling for $2.23/gal. In San Angelo, the average price for diesel was $3.36/gal. The combined state and federal tax for diesel in Texas is 44.4 cents per gallon. That's almost a 20% tax based on the crude price. Just the combined cost of the crude and the tax at the pump results in $2.674/gal. This results in a gross margin of $0.686/gal. difference between the crude and retail.

From this sixty-eight or so cents per gallon margin, subtract transportation costs (truck & pipeline), to get the crude to the refinery, then to the retail outlet. An estimate of $0.15/gal for transportation leaves a margin of about fifty three cents per gallon for all of the costs of refining and marketing. The refinery has a large investment (possibly in the hundreds of millions) and pays property tax, insurance, wages, repairs, various operating costs, then the finished product must be transported to a retail outlet. The retail store also has a large investment in facilities, tanks, pumps and credit card payment systems. The retail store pays property tax, insurance, wages and various operating expenses.

One of the old arguments is that diesel and gasoline are just by-products and that the other products like motor oil, grease, plastics and synthetic materials are where the real profit is made. From personal observation, we use at least a few gallons of diesel and gasoline every day compared to the equivalent of only a few drops of other petroleum based products. A 1:1 ratio of the comparison of crude to refined product is not completely accurate, but it does provide a comparison.

Do you remember when the fuel tax was posted on the fuel pumps? Many of us remember when diesel prices were lower than what the taxes are now. A tax of $.444/gal on diesel priced at $3.36/gal results in a tax rate of just over 13%. One chart showed that the tax was fifteen cents/gal thirty years ago which was probably about the same percentage rate as it is today. It is interesting to note that the fuel tax is a fixed rate per gallon rather than a percentage. If it had been set at a percentage, then the taxes would have increased right along with the price of fuel. However, the taxes would have decreased if and when the price went down which might have caused great consternation among bureaucrats and politicians. It would be interesting to know why they quit posting the amount of tax on fuel pumps.

The news media seems to have an envious delight about reporting the profits made by oil companies but seldom complains about high tech companies or celebrities income. It seems that the reports will usually be prefaced with the term "huge" or "obscene" but will seldom show the actual return on investment. A recent report showed that Exxon dividends are about 2.7%. Most of the oil producing and refining companies put a significant portion of earnings back into exploration and development.

It's difficult to get the exact numbers on the costs of production and refining since most of that information is proprietary. It probably varies from one company to another and may change daily. The advantage of the oil company is that they have a market for their product every day. Unlike the beef producer whose cow produces only one calf per year and there for has a product for sale only one day per year per cow. Just remember that it is the same reporters talking about big oil profits who are talking about ranchers now making large profits with the high beef prices.

Usually, when asked about why diesel prices are so high, I simply skip the analytical aspect and give the answer that never provokes an argument: "They are making OLD MEN work in the oilfield and we have no mercy and will charge all we can."

LW36...OIL ABOUT RANCHING...OVERRIDES

A lady who I've known most of my life called and asked about a situation regarding oil royalties that she had inherited from her parents. She is very smart, highly educated, lives in a big city and we may visit about once every five years or so. She told me that she didn't know anything about the oil and gas business and thought that the oil company was taking advantage of her due to her lack of knowledge. Sometimes I don't pick up on things right quick, but I knew instantly that she was very upset. Not at me but at the situation.

She had seen a document called the "Division Order" which itemized all of the oil production payment distribution regarding the property that she inherited. Her main concern was that some individuals were receiving what is called an "override" of the production from the wells on that property. She was concerned that these overrides were taking something away from her royalty interest and that some of the people getting an override of 1% or 2% were getting almost as much from the production as she was receiving.

In answer to her request to explain override, I told her that my understanding was that an override paid the stated percentage based on production, before expenses, similar to the way that royalty payments are made. An override might be paid in lieu of a cash payment to someone who performed a specific service on the well, such as the person who secured the lease. A person receiving an override would only get paid if and when the well produces. In that case, the person accepting the override is taking some risk and the operator is reducing his cash outlay. The difference in an override and a "working interest percentage" is that the working interest owner participates in both the expenses and income.

An independent operator may have several investors in a well and these may all be "working interest owners". The working interest owners could, if they so choose, negotiate with a service provider to take an override that might provide some income in the future. The override should come out of the working interest owner percentage and should have no impact on the royalty owner.

In this case, she told me that she and her sister had inherited 50% of the royalty interest. The lease agreement was that the royalty payments would be one-eighth, or 12.5%, of which she and her sister would get one-half, or 6.25% when divided equally with her sister, her percentage is 3.125%. Upon review of her check stubs, she stated that is exactly the percentage that she is being paid.

She was relieved to know that she was receiving proper payment and was embarrassed that she hadn't done a little number crunching and checked the bottom line percentages. The conversation ended with her being in a much better mood than when it started.

Another situation was brought up by a gentleman who owns some land in close proximity to my residence. There is one well on the property, producing about ten or eleven barrels per day. This is a very interesting well where I observed the completion attempts and never saw any indication of hydrocarbons. The well was declared dry and the operator started the application process to turn it into a disposal well. Before the change was made, the lease was sold to another operator who decided that he would put a pumping unit on the well and just give it a chance and see if it had any possibility. It didn't produce anything for several days and then began producing about a barrel per day and gradually increased up to eleven barrels per day. We all laugh that it is the best dry hole we've seen.

His question involved the erratic payments that he was receiving. He said that one month the check would be twice as much as the previous month and then down again the next month. He was curious about what could be causing this fluctuation. The pumper had told me that with the production at 10-11 bbls/day, it would average about one and one-half truck loads of oil per month and that one month they would sell two truck loads of oil and the next month only one. The monthly fluctuations averaged out for the year.

It was a reminder that every business has its own language and sometimes it takes only a little effort to bridge the gap of understanding.

LW37...OIL ABOUT RANCHING...CHRISTMAS, THIRTY YEARS AGO

The latest report that I read showed that the U.S. rig count is up by 12 from the previous week. That is further evidence that we did not have the "fourth quarter slump" that some predicted. Oil is slightly above $97 per barrel. Word came in that an operator in the Permian Basin is picking up an additional six horizontal rigs. Looks like the oil boom is still going strong.

The recent cold snap with sleet and freezing rain brought memories of the really bad cold spell here in west central Texas thirty years ago. In one conversation, the question came up about what year it was that broke all records. I told them it was 1983, but they weren't sure. I told them that I was absolutely sure because I got married two days before Christmas in 1983. I was working on a well near Big Piney, Wyoming that winter and it was colder at Winters, Texas the day of the wedding.

The fact we are about to celebrate our thirtieth anniversary, is evidence that miracles do occur and that my wife, Audine, has a high tolerance and adaptability level. Some people tell me that I'm the luckiest guy in the world to be married to her and wonder why a beautiful young lady would ever have anything to do with a cowboy who works in the oilfield? Full disclosure: I told her that the oilfield was hard, dirty and dangerous and so were most of the people involved in it. That didn't scare her away. She was impressed that I had owned the same horse for twelve years.

For her, it has undoubtedly been a challenge. She

has seen me get called to work unexpectedly (until the unexpected became the expected), saw me knocked unconscious in a horse wreck in Ft. Worth, been through a few oil field booms and busts, then selling cattle a couple of times due to drought. She has risen above it all and has been a great mom for our only child, Roy, who is a pilot and currently working as a flight instructor.

Audine made some quick adjustments. When we married she was teaching school at Winters and I was working as a company man for big oil on a well in Wyoming, working a seven on, seven off schedule making weekly flights. I had warned her that the oilfield was a little unpredictable. About six weeks later, I came home as scheduled on a Tuesday. On Wednesday night, my boss called and said that he "handled a personnel matter" and that he needed me back on the rig and that he would be taking care of things until I got there. That meant that if I was already on a plane headed north, I was late. Caught the first flight out of Abilene the next morning. So, I finished the rest of his hitch and then did mine. Welcome to the oil patch.

At the time we married, I had some cattle in a feedlot at Pecos and they were contracted at a nice profit. We drove out one winter week-end to see the cattle. She had never been right inside a big feedlot. Since it was cold, the windows were up and the smell had not permeated the car. As Audine stepped out of the car, she exclaimed "Wow! The smell!" We had bought a little house and were fixing it up and I just responded that it smelled like new carpet and a washer and dryer. She replied, "Not so bad once you get used it." How's that for a quick adjustment?

When big oil turned out the lights in the Midland office, there was a slight possibility that I might be offered a job in Houston, but Audine said that the old house in the country looked better than anything she had seen in Houston. With her attitude, I knew it would be okay. We had been married just over ten years and were packing to move. I came in and she held up a book of Ace Reid "Cowpoke" cartoons and said that she had just gone through those cartoons and realized that they are REAL and went on to say that she would have understood me better if she had read that before we married.

Audine is a teacher who is gifted with a love for children. Her work involves children who have difficulties in learning to read. Last week she said that a girl who she had worked with for three years, and is now in the fifth grade, came by to tell her that she had made the "A" honor roll. Since her work involves students with special needs, the confidentiality is such that I do not know which children are her students until some parent tells me what a great job that she has done with their child. She is doing her part to change the world, one child at a time. All I do is disturb livestock and drill holes in the ground.

Cold weather is not fun for people involved in the oil or ranching business. This cold spell brought back a lot of memories and it seems timely as our thirtieth anniversary approaches. For those of you who I've never met, I wanted to share a little history and let you know that I really have been involved with livestock and oil for a while. Here's hoping you have a wonderful Christmas, some great memories and continue to extend the faith and values into the next generation. Let's get ready to produce some more oil and beef next year.

LW39...OIL ABOUT RANCHING...COLD

When asked about how I liked the recent two day cold spell where it dropped to a low of eleven degrees, my response is that of being thankful that through it all we running water, a warm house, no interruptions in electricity and very glad that I'm not working on a drilling rig in the northern states. My compliments and sympathy to those who work in areas where it stays below zero for weeks.

On the days that it is below freezing in the Permian Basin, I would prefer to be on a Wyoming rig because they prepare for the cold weather. They know that when it gets cold they are in it for the long haul. The boiler is a necessity, not just a luxury. Steam lines running from the boiler to the rig floor, dog house, mud room and up to the derrick board help to make it tolerable. That is much better than just some tarps around the rig floor area. Being acclimated to the cold weather surely makes a difference, but preparation is the key to success and survival.

Several people have asked the question about whether it really makes any difference how much lower the temp drops once it gets below zero. My feelings are that every few degrees colder makes a difference. Metal frames on glasses become intolerable. Breathing through a wool scarf becomes a requirement for survival rather than just a creature comfort to avoid breathing cold air that is uncomfortable. Somewhere around 20 below zero it becomes dangerous to breathe the cold air directly. At those temps, the buddy system is used so that nobody is outside without someone being aware of where they are and what they are doing. It goes from cold to "scary cold".

When drilling at 9,000' elevation in Wyoming, the coldest temperature that I witnessed was 42 below zero, real temperature before wind chill factor. Fortunately, there was not a high wind at that time. Logistics of getting personnel, materials and equipment in and out become the major consideration. It is absolutely imperative that adequate rig and boiler fuel are maintained with a significant margin for safety factor. For weeks, there was a D8 Cat running 24 hours a day to be ready for falling or blowing snowstorms. If it was turned off and allowed to cool down completely at those temperatures, it might not start, so was kept running continuously. The wrong blend of diesel left some trucks stranded because the fuel turned to gel. Late one afternoon, after having been involved with several weather related issues, I realized that I had not even thought about the drilling operation all day. The driller would have notified me of any problems, but it was somewhat disturbing that the drilling of the well had been relegated to a lower priority.

Many of those who were native to the high country and cold winters told me that they preferred the cold weather because it was possible to put on enough clothes to stay warm but it's impossible to take off enough to stay cool. One man working in the cold environment was a native of Hawaii and he said that he enjoyed the cold weather and big changes in the seasons because the weather in Hawaii was boring because it was about the same all the time. One summer while doing some work near Gillette, Wyoming a rancher asked me if I was familiar with Del Rio. He said that was where he spent the winter and let his boys take care of the ranch in Wyoming. Even some of the natives can stand only so much of the cold weather.

The cattle grow much longer hair and an "ice cap" on their back was something to see. Somebody told me that it had an igloo effect and helped to keep them from freezing. Water lines are buried more than six feet deep and there were many days without sunshine. It was quite an adjustment, even though it was temporary, for someone who was raised south of Interstate 20.

In the recent cold spell, several news outlets reported that some oil drilling and production had been interrupted or suspended due to the extreme cold weather and that supplies may be affected and there could be shortages and price increases. That ranks right there with the reports that cattle in feedlots may not gain as well during severe weather and that beef supplies may be affected resulting in rising beef prices. Thanks to good planning and preparation, most of the operations will see the cold weather as an expected inconvenience and be back to normal in a few days.

Working in the Rocky Mountains in the summer was a wonderful experience. The winter time was a learning experience and one thing of which I am absolutely certain; it's more fun to write about the experiences of those cold temperatures than to think about going through the experience again. (From the never say never file: During the writing of this article, I received a call about going to a rig in the Texas panhandle.) It's good that I hung on to that cold weather clothing.

LW40...OIL ABOUT RANCHING...CATTLE GUARDS

While at the WRCA Ranch Rodeo finals in Amarillo, a rancher from the Fort Worth area told me about how an oil company was very agreeable and accommodating where he had some grass leases. They had put in cattle guards with gates beside the cattle guard, just as he had requested. He said that everything looked great until he drove up one day and found two cows stuck in a cattle guard. The thing that really upset him was that nobody told him about it. We agreed that one cow might wander into a cattle guard but for two there was probably some pressure on them. Somebody probably saw it happen and then had to go around the cattle guard and through the gate.

The person who saw but did not report the cows caught in the cattle guard may have had a lot of experience as the recipient of "shoot the messenger syndrome" and did not want to be a target again. It was much less painful to ignore it than report it. Most people would probably have reported the incident of the cows. Again, we're probably dealing with the 80/20 scenario where 20 percent of the people cause 80 percent of the problems. It's also possible that the person who caused the problem was not involved in any way with the oil company and was not authorized to be on that property. But the oil company or drilling contractor seem to always be the ones to be blamed for any incident.

Our conversation opined that today only a very small percentage of people have had any real livestock experience. At a cattle raisers meeting, a situation was discussed about an auction company and a cow that had somehow escaped and was causing some confusion on the roadway. A misunderstanding with a deputy made the situation worse. It was later pointed out by the sheriff that it was no longer a country town and that there was probably only one or two deputies on the force of a dozen or so who had ever had any livestock experience.

The lack of livestock experience is something that has really changed in a generation or so. When I was in school, it seemed that the majority of kids had grandparents or aunts and uncles who had a farm or ranch where they had the opportunity to have some kind of livestock experience and learn some respect and maybe some fear of farm animals. It's a reminder of what can be lost in just one generation.

In Canada, I saw a sign on the highway that stated "Texas Gate Ahead". My first thought was that it was a wire gap that was fiddle string tight and didn't have a cheater to help get it open. At Belle Creek, Montana, a man giving directions used the term "auto gate" which made me think "automatic gate". I asked him how it worked and he looked at me sort of funny and said, "You just drive right across it". Instead of asking any more questions, I hoped that I could figure it out when I got there. Sure enough, in both cases it was what I describe as a cattle guard.

LW41...OIL ABOUT RANCHING...TIGHT HOLE

West Texas Intermediate crude was trading just over $97 per barrel during the last week of January. A man in Midland who provides technical service to the oilfield told me that it looked like drilling activity would continue to increase as long as there is one more rig available to put to work. He recently flew over the busiest area of the Permian Basin and said that there is an unbelievable amount of activity. There is a lot going on but it's difficult to get all the information we desire.

A feedlot manager told a rancher that he could not give him the performance information on a particular pen of cattle, because those cattle belonged to another person. The customer who fed those cattle is the one who PAID for that information and it belonged to him. A similar thing occurs in the oilfield. The company putting up the money is the one who is assuming all of the risk and has expectations that the knowledge gained from the experience may be of value in the future. Sometimes on a wildcat well, a company may be experimenting with various processes or technology and may be interested in obtaining more leases in the area "if" things look good.

When a company is keeping all of the information close to vest, the well is called a "tight hole" and only designated people get any information. The worst thing about a "tight hole" is that when word gets out that it is a tight hole, curiosity kicks into overdrive. It seems like it's a lot easier to keep a secret, when there is no appearance of trying to keep something secret.

As a drilling consultant, I am often asked if we've seen any oil yet and if it's going to be a good well. If it's a "tight hole" I tell them that I am not allowed to give out any information on the well. When I tell them that I don't know if a well is going to be good or not, the look in their eyes usually indicates that they believe that I know something that I'm not telling. Asking someone during a drilling operation how good a well is going to be is very much like asking whether a particular yearling colt is a going to win the NCHA or All-American Futurity. It's still a while before anyone will know that information.

The drilling rig gets the attention but is usually long gone before anybody really knows what a well is going to produce. The completion and testing may take several weeks. It's not simply a case of just drilling into the right zone and finding oil. There are still many variables to get the oil out of the ground. The really hot areas where nearly every well is a good, leaves the impression that all you have to do is just drill a hole in the ground until oil is found. Different areas and different formations require different completion programs and it is still not an exact science.

Unfortunately, some people will try to read between the lines only to discover that the problem with reading between the lines is that there is nothing there. Many times the people who appear to be in a position to know something, really may not know anything. If they have some good indicators, they may not want to share their opinion on their limited info because they do not want to give somebody false hope.

On one occasion, my vantage point was horseback so I was close enough to see and hear some of what was going on. (My Donaho saddle was new back then and I was a lot younger.) The prospects for a gas well appeared much better than average. The couple who owned the property, and minerals, had reason to be excited when the drilling rig moved in. Their hopes were strengthened by the fact that there were producing wells just across the fence to the north and also to the west. The woman made the statement that she sure was not going to spend any of that gas money until it was in the bank. It appeared that she changed her mind and some car salesman along the river on the southern border must have been in full agreement with her decision to spend some of that gas money that was sure to be coming in. The well turned out to be a dry hole and I heard that it took her a long time to pay for that yellow Oldsmobile.

That was one of the observations that led me to believe that the only way to know if a well is a good one is when the check clears the bank.

LW43...Oil About Ranching...Mohair

It must have been those mohair socks worn during the recent cold weather that caused me to think about a possible application for mohair fabric. Okay, I'll admit that I'm prejudiced toward Angora goats. When I was five years old, I raised an orphan goat on a bottle. I remember getting $2.50 for the mohair at shearing time. I once told a banker that mohair was what got me started on my first million and that I was still working on it but mohair was where it started!

In todays "kinder gentler" oilfield, one of the major complaints is about the requirement to wear "FRC- flame resistant clothing" in many locations. Most of these consist of cotton clothing that has been treated with some type of chemical, or a patented fabric that has the not natural fabric feel about it. The similarities are that both types are about three times more expensive than traditional work clothes and have the conductive capability of some polyester fabrics that feel colder in the winter and hotter in the summer. Is it possible that a mohair blend would have been better?

Several workers have commented that they do not know of one individual who has been involved in a flash fire situation where they needed the protection of fire resistant clothing but they all know of people who have suffered from heat exhaustion blamed partially on the effects of the FRC clothing. Bear in mind that these complaints are coming from people who do not complain about wearing hard hats, steel toed boots and gloves for protection. But questioning any safety rule is treading on treacherous ground. It seems that the rule makers always add more rules but never take any away.

The lack of information pertaining to the required FR clothing is somewhat disturbing. What was the comparison? Was it compared to an all cotton product or to polyester or some blend? Was the effectiveness two percent better or two hundred percent? It seems that I remember something about requirements in aviation many years ago for mohair carpet due to the flame resistant qualities. Many welders prefer to wear a leather welding jacket, some of which are made with metal staples or brass rivets rather than being stitched with thread which may burn out. It would be interesting to know how these patented "FRC processes" would compare to mohair blends and to leather. It would be interesting to know about any research that has been done using mohair fabric.

The thoughts of mohair caused me to think about the comparison of price changes of oil and of mohair. A little informal research back to the 70's revealed some mohair at thirty cents a pound. That must have been at a low time for the market but not the worst. I remember in the sixties, when I was in high school, that my Dad had three clips of mohair in the warehouse with "no bid". At some point there was simply no market. At the time that mohair was thirty cents a pound, oil was under government controls at about three dollars per barrel. I do not remember the details of the wool and mohair incentive program, but do remember that it seemed to be an effective program to level the playing field in the competition of imported products. When the wool and mohair incentive program was eliminated, those natural fabrics and the producers took a major economic hit. At least some of us can say that with the wool and mohair incentive program and the screwworm eradication, we have seen two government programs which actually proved successful for the intended purpose.

If mohair prices had maintained parity with oil prices, it looks like mohair would be somewhere near eighteen dollars per pound. In that case, Angora numbers would probably have increased rather than been in a steep decline. A lot of the brush country would be trimmed up nicely and the aquifers under it might be much better.

Speaking of water; I am hearing about more oil and gas operators who are using some produced water (water that is produced along with the oil) and re-using flow back water in their frac operations. It's a matter of conservation and economics to re-use the water. Still haven't heard anything about any municipalities mandating restrictions which would require all new construction to have rain water catch systems or to have gray water systems to re-use water for flushing. Water conservation may someday be elevated to a higher priority.

LW44...OIL ABOUT RANCHING...POOLING AGREEMENTS

A friend sent a question about an oil and gas lease for a few acres that would be involved in a pooling agreement. First of all, I did the usual disclaimers about not offering legal advice, not a lawyer, don't play one on TV or dress up and pretend to be one on weekends.

My earliest memory of a discussion about pooling agreements was hearing a neighbor say "Never get in a pool". I did not understand what they were talking about, but the strong statement stuck in my memory. Many years later, I learned some of the benefits of "Never say never". A pooling agreement may be a good thing. The acreage in discussion is a case where pooling is possibly a very good thing because it may be the only way to lease the property.

The owner has about seven acres and the oil company is interested in leasing the acreage but seven acres, by itself, is not enough acreage to acquire a permit to drill and produce oil. The oil company desires to put together a forty acre tract in the pooling agreement in order to have sufficient acreage for drilling. The oil company is putting a puzzle together. Each tract involved should receive proceeds equivalent to the percentage of the acreage involved.

Without going into a pooling agreement, there is possibly no way that they can lease the property. They have the opportunity to participate in something that may be mutually beneficial with their neighbors or they can refuse to participate and get nothing and maybe cause their neighbors to also get nothing. I have been involved in a lease where I owned less than two percent of the mineral interest and the last thing that I would want to do is to mess up the lease for the majority. I've known of situations where somebody held out for just a little more and ended up with a whole bunch of nothing. I am all too familiar with one lease where the oil company evidently gave up on finding the owners of the remaining 13% of the royalty and did not renew the lease for the 87% which they had put together.

It appears that leasing the seven acres as part of the pool to make up the forty acres is a good opportunity to go along to get along with the neighbors. It's probably not an opportunity to get rich but it may be an opportunity to participate in something that may bring in a few dollars.

The lease involving the seven acres clarified some very important things. Specifically it stated that the lease did not involve anything pertaining to the surface and that no entries, locations, roads, easements or pipelines would be allowed on the surface portion involving those specified seven acres. That sounded really good that the surface portion of that acreage would not be disturbed and no damages would be incurred.

No mention was made about how close this might be to any residences, businesses or schools. There might be some legitimate reason that a property owner did not want any drilling activity in that area and could refuse to lease their portion in an attempt to prohibit drilling. The scenario might exist that the company desiring to lease the property might be able to lease something on the opposite side of the tract. That might just shift the position and put together a slightly different puzzle of forty acres and leave out the seven acre tract. A hard nosed negotiator might just get left out if their demands are extreme.

It's been over thirty years ago and I won't reveal the name of a hard nosed negotiator who bluffed himself out of a nice check. The oil company needed to lay a temporary fresh water line across a few miles of some creosote brush desert country. The worst or actually best case scenario would be in the event of a leak in the fresh water line anywhere in that dry ranchland. Instead of accepting the "typical going rate" for access and damages, the rancher demanded a payment of four times that amount. Somebody in the claims and right of way group of the company decided to do a little more research.

It just so happened that the ranch in question did not own all of the acreage that was within the fence boundaries. It was a checkerboard of owned and non-owned acreage under one fence. As it turned out the oil company had an access easement in place regarding the non-owned acreage within the ranchers fence boundaries and did not have to pay for access or damages to lay a poly line for temporary use. They ended up agreeing to pay the rancher for the amount that he wanted per foot to cross his land. They shot the gap across a corner in the checkerboard and paid him his requested rate for only one foot, instead their normal rate for two miles. It made me wonder how many times that he may have collected for damages that were not due to him and if he had bluffed so many times that he forgot that he was bluffing. Some famous horse trader said that greed can be a terrible thing.

LW45...OIL ABOUT RANCHING...PRODUCTION UP

West Texas Intermediate Crude Oil was slightly above $102 per barrel during the first week of March 2014. Drilling permits for Texas in December 2013 were about ten percent above the number for December 2012. The optimism indicated by the increase in drilling permits appears to be paying off based on the increase in the price of oil.

According the Texas Railroad Commission, the 2013 production for Texas was just over 704 million barrels which was seventeen percent above the production for 2012 and more than double the average production for the years 2007-09. Oil production in 2013 added about $10 billion dollars to the Texas economy compared to 2012. That is actual dollars and does not include any "multiplier effect" of the money being circulated through the economy. Compared to five years ago, that number is about $35 billion increase. This country continues to import a significant amount of oil so the economic impact may be double because every additional barrel of oil produced is one less that is imported.

Some economists could probably explain the multiplier effect that the increase in oil production is having on both local and the national economy. In some areas, the impact of the oil boom is all too obvious but by driving a few miles to the next small town outside of the oil boom area there is no indication of an economic boom. It is easy to talk about the growth of some local economies but there is some downside because of the inflation and traffic congestion that comes with the increased activity.

The activity in the oil patch indicates that much of the profit is being reinvested in more drilling and infrastructure. More and better roads are needed in the areas where drilling and production are very active. The roads are a real dilemma. By the time something has to be done to improve the roads, traffic congestion will only be made worse by the construction zones. In talking about the traffic problems in the Permian Basin, I told someone that they just needed to drive out and see how bad the traffic really is on the roads, but then I changed that and told them to not drive those roads unless they absolutely must. Reports are that it is every bit as bad in South Texas and North Dakota. If you want to look at the activity, it's probably a lot safer to fly over it than drive through it.

Speaking of flying. My son is a flight instructor and has been doing flying lessons for a few men in Big Lake. He noticed an unexpected benefit from some of the oil activity that was created by seismic crews cutting paths through some of the pastures covered with brush. These pathways create a large grid visible from the air and can be used to show the effect of wind and the drift that can occur in turns. Having spent many hours on an excavator clearing brush during the summer when he was sixteen, he was very appreciative of the effort that went into creating that large grid. That was also the time that he re-evaluated his desire to be a heavy equipment operator.

One of the comments that I hear frequently is accusing companies of hiring just anyone they can find and putting them in a big truck. When an unlicensed driver of a big rig is involved in an accident, it makes the news and also leaves the indication that this is a widespread problem. This is a problem that is NOT being ignored by much of the petroleum industry. Many of the companies are now putting a great deal of effort into maintaining an "approved vendor" list. The safety record and programs to improve safety are very important aspects considered before adding a company to the approved vendor list. As someone who is often working and traveling in the midst of it, safety is very important to me and I am glad to know that at least parts of the industry are not ignoring the situation.

A recent report showed that North Dakota was the "happiest" state in the nation. They did not report how the survey was taken but maybe they surveyed a hundred people and half of them had a new oil well and half of them had just sold a load of calves for over thousand dollars a head. Not saying that money will buy happiness, but for some of us who have ridden the ups and downs in both the oil and ranching business it is really nice to be riding on the top of the wave right now. Some of us are just like the kid with a big bowl of ice cream who is concerned that it may melt before he can eat it all. We better enjoy the moment and try not to get a brain freeze.

LW46...OIL ABOUT RANCHING...CLOSED LOOP SYSTEM

One reader asked for me to write about "closed loop systems" and the effect that these systems may have on reducing surface damage and the footprint that may be left when the drilling operations are completed. First, let's look at some of the basic processes of a drilling operation in order to explain the closed loop system for those who have never heard the term.

As a well is being drilled, the drill bit basically scrapes and/or crushes the rock into small particles which are called cuttings. These are flushed from the well bore with water and drilling mud. In some areas the wells are drilled with air and the cuttings are blown out with the air pressure. Since most wells are drilled using water and drilling mud, that will be the example used here. Due to formation pressure, (which is the pressure exerted due to the weight of the formation), it is expected that most of the zones will be a rock like substance due to this compressive factor.

Normal formation pressure is described as the weight of fresh water multiplied times the standard pressure gradient multiplied by the depth. Fresh water, weighing 8.3 pounds per gallon multiplied by the gradient 0.052 multiplied by the depth, for example 1,000' would result in a formation pressure of a little over 430 pounds per square inch. Several other factors contribute to the hardness of a formation but for simplicity the point is that most of the drilling is done through a rock like substance and these rock chips are circulated to the surface.

As the drilling mud is circulated from the well bore, it goes across a screened shaker system that is vibrating which facilitates the fluid to pass through the screen and be re-circulated and the cuttings roll of the end of the shaker and go to the reserve pit. For several decades, this has been the accepted practice and the cuttings from a well bore remain on that site and are covered or blended in with the topsoil as the area is re-claimed.

The so-called "closed loop system" is touted as an improvement in the method because all of the cuttings are hauled away from the well site and disposed at some other location. Also, in most cases this eliminates the reserve pit so there is less area to be reclaimed. In theory, all of the potential contamination is being removed from site. This is probably an ideal solution for some areas, involving certain soil types, water zones that are permeable easily from surface leaching and the rock chemistry that may have negative effects with the topsoil. So, the closed loop can eliminate some problems and should be an easy sell, right? With the right buzz word, such as "reduce the footprint" you can sell almost any idea to the green crowd. From a cattleman's perspective, you might compare this idea to "COOL" (Country of Origin Labeling) and serilously examine the details before accepting the idea as a cure all that should be applied everywhere.

A big difference is that the closed loop system can be applied selectively rather than a one size fits all. However, in some areas it has been applied absolutely with no exceptions. "Closed loop" has a nice sound to it, like something is being contained and controlled. Hauling something away seems to be a readily accepted, one dimensional solution. This begs the following questions: Where is it being hauled? Does concentrating numerous small quantities into a large disposal (reverse dilution?) create more problems than it solves? What about the carbon footprint and the increased traffic and related hazards of all those trucks hauling the cuttings? And, follow the money and ask who is making a profit from the process and who is paying lobbyists to push the agenda?

There are some operational considerations about eliminating reserve pits. For instance, a problem may arise during the process of pumping cement around the casing. When a problem arises while pumping cement, it requires a quick decision because cement must be kept moving if at all possible. In some cases, the cement must be circulated out so that corrective action may be implemented to re-do the cement job. If the cement is circulated out, there must be some place for it to go other than the metal holding tanks. There are other reasons to have at least a minimal size, emergency reserve pit. Eliminating one so called problem may eliminate the ability to deal with another real problem.

Recently, it was brought to my attention that there is some study being done about cleaning the cuttings and using them as base material for roads and locations. It sounds like this could be a win/win situation to have beneficial use of a waste product which could also reduce the need for surface mining of caliche and rock crushing for road base material. It may turn out that the best case scenario is to use a closed loop system and use the cuttings for base material.

I have gathered cattle afoot, horseback, with a feed sack and with a helicopter and can argue in favor of each method under particullar circumstances. Most of all I am thankful that no bureaucrat or legislative body has taken it upon themselves to mandate that we can gather cattle using only their "approved" method. It is probably human nature that we are all suspicious of any industry in which we have absolutely no knowledge. Ask yourself the question pertaining to whatever industry in which you are invested: Do you trust someone from outside your industry to be the one to fix something which may not be broken?

Closed loop systems may be a really good idea for many applications. One size may not fit all. The cost and risk in some cases may grossly outweigh the benefits. It may be the cool thing to do, or not.

LW47...Oil About Ranching...The First Anniversary (4-5-2014)

If you can imagine watching your favorite pro team for forty years and suddenly have an opportunity to suit up and go into a game, then you have some idea how I felt about the opportunity to write for the Livestock Weekly,(after being a subscriber for about forty years). My first thought was that I simply did not have the time for it because I do work as a drilling consultant spending days and nights on drilling rig sites being available twenty four hours per day during my hitch. However, I did not want to pass up the opportunity to "get in the game" with something that I've respected for a long time. My goal is to help bridge the gap of understanding between ranchers and the oilfield. This marks one year since this column originated. I want to thank Bobby Frank for the opportunity.

On more than one occasion, I've been at some function and a friend who I haven't seen for quite some time says hello and then introduces me to someone beside them saying that I am the one who writes the "Oil About Ranching" column in the Livestock Weekly. It's both exciting and humbling to have something of a new identity. It's exciting that they are subscribers and know that the other party also reads the column. One gentleman to whom I had been introduced told me that he reads the column and immediately followed with "But I still miss Elmer Kelton". My response was "Don't we all", followed by saying that he was setting the bar a little bit too high for me to compare with that legend. It is more than just a little intimidating to think of who used to write on these pages; Stanley Frank,

Elmer Kelton and Monte Noelke whose columns and books that I enjoyed.

The only opportunity that I had to visit with Elmer Kelton was at a book signing many years ago. During that short visit, I thanked him for writing the book "Honor At Daybreak" (about the early oil field) and how much that I identified with some of the characters who went from the ranch to the oilfield and especially one statement that went something like this: "I haven't gotten rich in the oilfield like some people, but I've had a front row seat to one of the greatest shows on earth." Now we are seeing one of the biggest oil booms in history just a short time after the petroleum industry had been declared a mature industry, on the decline, with no new fields left to discover.

It seems like I'm often answering questions in the oil field about why do ranchers and farmers do something a certain way. When I'm around my friends and neighbors in agriculture, I get many questions about the oilfield. Many of those conversations have been the basis for these articles as well as comments and questions from those who read the column.

The most exciting thing for me about writing this column is meeting people who have read the columns and it's like we are old friends that had never met. For any new readers who might be wondering about my background, I grew up on a modest ranching and farming operation, got a degree in Ag Economics then got hungry and went to work in the oil field. I've always maintained an active interest in livestock, (never sold my saddle) and now I'm back for about my fourth or fifth go round in the oilfield (never gave away my Halliburton book).

I worked for Big Oil for over sixteen years and then moved back to the country when they turned out the lights in my office in '94. As stated earlier, the oilfield was considered "matured" and the Permian Basin was used up. Since coming back to the oil patch, I've worked for some major companies and several independents, including one who should have been governor. In about three years, the place where we live will qualify to be recognized as one hundred years of continuous family operation. One of my goals is to use my experience on both sides of the fence to help bridge the gap of understanding between oil people and ranch people.

To say that I am blessed is an understatement. The past year has flown by. I want to say thanks for the encouragement from so many readers. Even the old friend who told me that he was reading the column and looked up to see who wrote it and was surprised that it was me! I told him that if he thought he was surprised, could he imagine the surprise of our senior English teacher, who told me that I could not handle college English. From a different perspective, I shall always be thankful for Prof. Feynn who told me that I should be a writer because the most important thing is to be able to communicate an idea and that punctuation and grammar were secondary to communication.

Questions and comments from readers are very important to me. This is a very exciting time with things happening very fast in the oil industry. The pace is frantic and in some areas the ranching industry and traditions are being changed forever, and maybe not for the better. Sometimes, my mind cannot process all that I see happening. No claims here to being a journalist. Just experience and observations from an opinionated and sometimes narrow perspective by someone who learned to rope by doctoring animals with screwworms. My hungry cows appreciate my oilfield job. Dry weather is an incentive to go to work.

Thanks again for all of the encouragement and support. From all that I see and hear, the drilling activity is continuing to increase.

LW51 OIL ABOUT RANCHING...FENCE BUILDING 101

It wasn't that they didn't care. They really did not understand. In preparation for a rig move, one of the many instructions given to the rig manager was to have the crew repair the fence around the reserve pit behind the rig. As is typical, to access the reserve pit, the net wire will be untied from the posts and over a few days becomes very much flattened. The two young men who were assigned the repair task are strong hard workers and have proved to be proficient at numerous tasks. Like most roughnecks, they don't hesitate to do hard dirty work.

They came to me, as the company rep on site, for approval of the work they had performed. They asked if it was okay. It wasn't. It was so bad that I didn't say anything, that in itself being a rare event when I actually keep my mouth shut when I don't know what to say. While looking at that sad bit of fence that was just sort of propped up with some of the net wire wadded into a mess, the realization hit me that they had probably done exactly what someone had taught them at some time. It's an understatement to say that they had definitely not been trained along the lines of Red Steagall's recording of "The Fence That Me and Shorty Built".

In some ways it was fortunate that this was a late start rig move and the trucks would not arrive for a couple of hours. With a simple response that maybe we should tighten it up a little, I went to my pick-up and got some fencing pliers. Most rig hands are mechanically inclined and are familiar with many types of tools. They were fascinated with the bull-nose fence pliers, so it was obvious that they had really never been taught the basics of fence building. By showing them how to straighten out wadded net wire by standing on the bottom wire and pulling on the top and driving in an angle brace, we were able to secure the short section of fence.

It had never been explained to these two men that a fence must be tight or it is not going to serve the intended purpose. While we were on that project, one of the men said something about the ranchers being real particular about their fences. I responded that most of them had learned how to build fences at a young age and know how to do it right and if it's not right, then it really bothers them.

It was a learning experience all the way around. They learned that it was important enough for me to show them how to do it right, even though teaching fence building is not really what I'm hired to do. It opened my eyes to the fact that they really did not know how it should be done. No doubt, many readers of this column remember who taught them that a fence must be straight and tight and what a special memory that is. There was a posthole that took several afternoons, when I was in high school, to chip through the rock. About thirty years later, it was difficult to let a dozer knock down that corner post when we replaced and repositioned some fences. Some lessons stick better than others.

The question that I hear most often in this current oil boom is: "Where are they going to get the workers to fill the jobs if these companies get more rigs?" The lack of experience is frightening in some situations. However, the enthusiasm of some of the young workers just starting out is fun to see. One young man, newly hired as a floor hand on a rig, told me with a big smile that he had been trying to get a job on that rig for six months. He was excited. His crew comes from several hundred miles away and they work 14 days on and 14 off and stay in a skid mounted bunk house on location. Some former military personnel seem to have found a home in the oilfield because they understand hard work, discipline and chain of command. Drilling companies can compete with college recruiters by offering jobs at good pay as opposed to student loans for training for jobs that may not exist. Not downplaying the need for education, but there is some serious competition going on right now.

According to the Texas Railroad Commission, January and February production was about 8% higher than the same period last year. A recent article in a financial website referred to the U.S. oil production having peaked about 1970 and declined almost steadily until 2008. The current increase in oil production indicates that the 1970 record will be surpassed sometime in 2014. Even with that record production, we are only producing slightly over fifty percent of what the nation consumes. There's still a substantial amount of oil being imported and energy independence may yet be several years away. It will be exciting to watch and see what new technology is going to be developed in the near future. But what we really need right now is rain.

LW52...Oil About Ranching...Ear Tags

It is funny to see how many problems are solved with cowboy logic using a low tech solution on a high tech problem. Most of the newer generation of drilling rigs have components and tools that are run by computers and joystick controllers. All of this results in a massive number of electrical and communication lines plus hydraulic and air lines to provide the power. This is all very impressive when it is all working as designed. One crossed up connection can wreak havoc. Most of the rigs are dismantled and moved on a frequent basis. It is no small chore to keep things in order and know the right location for each connection.

Recently, while becoming familiar with a new rig to which I had been assigned, something that seemed out of place caught my eye. On a panel where numerous lines were connected, there were rows of cattle ear tags. Somebody had zip tied the numbered tags to the lines and developed a very efficient and effective method of labeling the lines. Many times the lines will be labeled by using tape and a permanent marker. Often, this has about the same success as the rancher who only had some of the old dry sheep chalk and used that to write down the info of the day's livestock work on fence boards. The intent was to bring his pencil and note pad the next day and copy the notes. A nice rain that night wiped out all of the records. (I wonder how many people will claim ownership to that event?) The high visibility and durability of the ear tags is probably appreciated by everyone involved. Whoever came up with that idea probably did not learn it in some post graduate course.

Many people have the idea that the new technology will result in fewer workers being needed on each rig. Actually, new technology has probably created more jobs than it has eliminated in the drilling industry. For every labor saving device, there is a demand for higher technical abilities. Horizontal drilling is an example of new technology and that aspect brings on a team of four individuals on location who are specifically dedicated to monitoring and directing the position of the bit to assure that the wellbore is progressing according to plan. There is a support group back at the shop where tools are assembled and refurbished.

The drilling equipment must be maintained, serviced, disassembled moved and put together frequently. Technology has helped speed up the drilling process to the point that we are drilling wells in less than half the time it took several years ago. Drilling the wells in half the time does not mean that everything involved has been cut in half. Like any other situation In going from point A to point B, if it is done in half the time, that is an indication that the pace has doubled. There is not much time to catch our breath between one activity and the next. Plus the paper work seems to have reached epidemic redundancy with a critical mass that is out of control. Last week, a man told me that he was going to the office for a company meeting. I told him that they would give him a new form to fill out. He sent a text that evening telling me that I was right about getting a new form. At times the insatiable desire for information is overwhelming.

Some of the new technology is proving beneficial. One company where I did some contract work for a few months was really big into text messages. That was when it was necessary to upgrade to a phone with a keypad. One advantage was being able to create a template where the well name and detailed directions to the well could be entered and saved. That template can then be sent to anyone who needs directions. There is something about making five left turns to get to a well site that works better in writing than telling it over the phone. Yes, one of the locations required five left turns which exceeded 360 degrees and was beginning the spiral effect. The cowboy way would have been to cut across in a straight line but that would be too logical.

It seems like most wells are located so that you make at least a half circle around it before actually getting there. Some things simply defy logic. Must be a Murphy's Law about location directions. Ever notice that the rodeo arena is on the other side of town about ninety percent of the time?

What a relief it was that the ear tags used to mark the equipment were NOT insecticide tags. Then there might have been a HazMat situation. About the only hazardous material that is causing a problem right now is dust. If we sell the cows, will it rain before the check clears the bank?

LW53...OIL ABOUT RANCHING...PEAK OIL

Several years ago someone asked me about the subject of "Peak Oil". It was an unfamiliar term that made me curious enough to do some research. It seems to have started with a scientist with a major oil company in the 1950's who made some predictions pertaining to the time that United States oil production would reach its peak and then begin a steady decline. The prediction was that oil production in this country would peak in the early 1970's. The research and analysis proved to be accurate with the petroleum production having peaked somewhere in the 1970-73 timeframe.

The statistics vary slightly because some reports are based solely on oil production and others are based on a combination of oil, gas and distillates which are liquids that are derived from some of the natural gas. Having made a relatively accurate prediction which tracked the increase for almost twenty years and then began a steady decline after it peaked, the prediction seems to have been accepted by many as solid science. More followers seemed to have jumped on the bandwagon as the downward trend continued through the 1990's and on into the Twenty-first century.

Although the term "peak oil" was not something that I heard inside big oil in the early 90's, it seemed to be accepted that the oil business was a "mature" business and that it was on a steady decline with no more new discoveries to be made. According to many of the experts at the time, the Permian Basin was almost a has-been. It was quite a shock to many of us who had worked for big oil to learn that more than half of us would soon be out of work and that the "career path" and retirement with full benefits changed from a dream to a nightmare. Suddenly, we knew how the buffalo hunters and stage coach drivers felt.

The accuracy of Peak Oil predictions seemed to have accurately summarized the best geologic and engineering data available at that time. Oil and gas production and the businesses associated with it were in decline. The individuals who made those predictions should not be criticized for not having foresight into new technology any more than Henry Ford should be criticized for using carburetors instead of fuel injection systems. Now it is obvious that "fracking" changed everything and a new boom was created. It took a lot of engineers and O-rings to get from there to here.

"Fracking" is getting most of the well deserved credit for the increase in oil production. To the uninformed, it may appear that hydraulic fracturing is an overnight success story. However, it took several decades to perfect the technique. Some of the early frac jobs, seventy or eighty years ago, used nitro-glycerin to fracture the formation in an attempt to increase the permeability and allow oil to flow to the well bore. Using nitro-glycerin was very risky and it is impossible to forget the historical account of one well site where all of the workers were found dead as a result of a nitro glycerin malfunction. Just like many other things that we seem to take for granted today, the development of the fracking process was not easy and was not cheap.

Hydraulic fracturing was developed over the decades as engineers made progress in handling higher pressures. Meanwhile, others were working on the physics of using sand particles to prop up the formation. Getting the sand far back into the fractures was enhanced by someone who developed a gel type substance that had the right consistency to suspend and carry the sand while maintaining enough of the fluid characteristics to allow it to be pumped into the formation. Along with the right pressure and chemical combination, thousands of barrels of water are pumped into the formation. Who would have thought that pumping large volumes of water would free up an even larger volume of oil?

While enjoying some very good barbeque at the Texas and Southwestern Cattle Raisers gathering during the Western Heritage at Abilene, it occurred to me that there are many similarities to the "over night" success stories about developments in both the beef and oil businesses. Watching the construction feedlots on the high plains in the early 70's, followed by major beef packers finding export markets for various offal products that were previously waste products, it is obvious that it didn't suddenly just happen.

Research and development teams do not often get the credit that they deserve. TSCRA gives credit to the Beef Check off for finding and marketing new cuts of beef which add about $170 to the value of each calf. The formerly cheap cut of flank steak being elevated to top shelf fajita meat was about the only one that I knew about. The successes of the beef check off are probably very similar to the success of hydraulic fracturing. Most of the people working behind the scenes don't get much credit for what they have done and what appears to be an over-night success actually took a few decades.

With oil and gas production increasing over the past few years, a new prediction is that oil and gas production in the United States will hit a new high sometime in 2014. Hopefully, someone is crunching the numbers and will be able to accurately identify the month and possibly even the day that will occur. Maybe there will be some sort of a celebration on that day. A tribute to American ingenuity and dedicated work over the long haul. A new all time high for petroleum production in the United States is a victory for us all. Ranchers probably need to be reminded that many oil people who celebrate the occasion will do so by enjoying a good steak, hamburger or fajitas.

LW55...OIL ABOUT RANCHING...WELL CONTROL SCHOOL

Ranchers and farmers who spend considerable time and effort keeping up with the CEU's to maintain their private pesticide applicator's license can probably sympathize with the drilling consultants who are required to attend Well Control Certification every two years. A big difference is that the well control school lasts three or four days and the one in February cost $1,200. The motel rate was comparable to the sum spent in a somewhat extravagant place in Silicon Valley a few years ago. The one in Odessa was being remodeled and other than the rate had little to compare with the place in Silicon Valley.

The course is not put on by the Extension Service or any other government agency. It is a private company that is certified to provide training. Most drilling consultants are considered to be independent contractors so the training must be done on days off and all expenses are out of pocket and not re-imbursed by some company. Many tool pushers and drillers are required to have well control training and it is customary that their companies pay for the training.

Well control training is designed train people to prevent an uncontrolled flow of gas or fluid to the surface. Blow out preventers are installed on the rig for the purpose of controlling the well if needed. The importance of well control cannot be overstated. Blow outs are notorious for killing people and destroying equipment. As the realtor said, "The three most important things are location, location, location", on a drill site the most important things are well control, well control, well control.

My first well control school was in 1978 and I was on the payroll of big oil who maintained their own training facility and the only people who were allowed to teach well control were those who had been directly involved in a significant well control situation. The training facility had a real well that had been partially plugged back and dual strings of tubing had been installed in the well. The dual string allowed one string to be used to inject air or nitrogen into the well to induce what is called a "gas kick" to simulate a well control situation. The facility had mud pits, pumps, blow out preventers and chokes just like what is found on many drilling rigs. It was as close as possible to a real well situation. The type of equipment, where it was positioned, how it felt and the sounds that were made were all real.

The last few well control schools were taught in a conference room in a hotel or office building. The most recent instructor had never been anywhere close to an actual well control situation. He had been taught to teach and did a good job of covering the material but had no experience to back up the training material. The wellbore, pumps, mud pits, chokes and blow-out preventers were all neatly packaged in computerized simulators. If this sounds something like watching a video of somebody riding a mechanical bull at Billy Bobs compared to climbing the chute and pulling the bull rope on a head slinging bovine, then you may understand my thoughts on the situation.

Maybe it was just the luck of the draw, but I was the oldest person in the classroom, by twenty plus years. Observing the responses of the younger people in the class was interesting. Anyone who has done just a small amount of teaching would have readily picked up on the fact that some in the class just were not getting it. Dealing with volumes and pressures of liquids and gases gets into math and physics very quickly. One of the young men blurted out, "There is a REASON that I quit school. I'm not good at this stuff!" My guess is that he was hyper-active and had difficulties with reading and most of his schooling experience was miserable. He can probably work a twelve hour shift on a rig and be ready for more, if needed.

It was interesting to see how things changed with most of the students when they went to the computerized simulators. They are all part of the video game generation so the computerized simulators were not intimidating to them at all. It was a hands-on exercise and most of them performed very well. The question is, how will this work out in the real world? Many of the wells being drilled today must be fracked before they will produce oil or gas. These zones are typically under pressured prior to fracking and seldom have any type of well control situation. It's much different from working the deep wells of the Anadarko basin (early 80's) in an area where six rigs had burned. Some people seem to think that they don't have to be concerned with the possibility of a blow-out. Complacency can be a dangerous thing.

Three days of classroom time reminded me of many of the people who taught me along the way. There is not much evidence of companies making long range investments in training people. I often wish that I could be involved in some training programs to pass along and pay forward some of the benefits that I received from the experience of others before me. Not that I know so much, but I now have a realization of how much I don't know.

LW56...OIL ABOUT RANCHING...RENEWABLE ENERGY

Renewable energy as understood by the original "green" crowd. A good rain and a new baby calf. The rain re-energizes the soil and the grass will turn green and the miraculous digestive system of the cow will convert the grass to milk and the calf will have energy. Renewable resources all around us thanks to a few inches of topsoil and some rain. Rain came to a large area and we are very thankful.

Once again, the big event happened during a time of being away at a well site. The rain came. Some pictures sent by e-mail of formerly dry tanks now full of water and a new baby calf helped brighten the day. But it is still not like being there. It rained on the drilling rig, too. The Permian Basin is so dry that the rain was welcome even though it made some of the work more of a challenge. It was a time to drag that yellow slicker out of the tool box. It's only worn only on special occasions that come all too seldom.

Some of the articles about the new type renewable energy of the wind, solar and ethanol variety are very interesting but there seems to be a shortage of solid information. One article on wind energy was celebrating that the costs of wind energy systems have been reduced over the past few years and stated that wind energy projects now cost only about 8% more per kilowatt hour to construct than do natural gas powered generating plants. At first glance, this almost made it appear that the playing field is almost level. What it did not state was the fact that wind is not always available to turn the turbines but that a natural gas plant can be run at any time and all the time. Instead of just comparing the construction and equipment costs, the percentage of time that wind is sufficient should be included in the data. If sufficient wind is available only 50% of the time, the cost per kilowatt hour based on production would be double.

Not to be knocking wind energy, but it would be nice if reports made factual comparisons of costs and inputs including tax incentives. One report stated that wind energy accounted for seven percent of the electrical energy produced in Texas. Competition can be a wonderful thing and it is very good to have diversification in the energy business. A good sign that that the wind energy business is truly profitable will be when "the greedy oil companies" jump on the bandwagon and begin building wind farms.

One proponent for ethanol on a TV farm show was promoting the idea of gas pumps with an ethanol selector dial where the customer could dial in the percentage of ethanol desired. This sounds like a great idea because then we can "follow the money" and see how much more (or less) that fuel costs per gallon when the ethanol percentage increases. The speaker was also making requests for people to encourage Congress to provide more incentives for ethanol.

Several years ago there was a report that a process had been developed to utilize more of the raw materials in building solar panels. Recent information reports that the cost of solar panel construction has decreased by something like ninety percent over the past few years. It is interesting to see many small solar panels in use in the oil field for providing power for automation and communication systems. An employee at a battery store said that a small solar panel costing less than $20 would be adequate to maintain the charge on a battery in a portable welder that might not be used for several weeks. He suggested something larger for a travel trailer with larger and more batteries.

Solar energy is phenomenal but the industry still hasn't done what nature does with sunlight providing chlorophyll to put the energy into the green plant so the cow can produce the milk. Science still has a way to go before turning sunshine into milk. With beef and oil being in high demand, it indicates that we still need to keep doing things the old fashioned way and let the cattle turn grass into beef to feed the people who are drilling the wells.

A short note informed me of something better than a good rain and new baby calf. A baby boy was born to a young couple in Glasscock county during a recent rainstorm. His name is Asa and I'm looking forward to meeting him.

LW57...OIL ABOUT RANCHING...RIG COUNT UP AGAIN

The U.S. rig count for May was 1,857 (including 1,783 on land, 14 working inland waters and 58 in the Gulf of Mexico) compared to 1,762 one year ago. More than two-thirds of these are reported to be horizontal projects which typically are the equivalent of drilling several vertical wells. By drilling the equivalent of several wells from one location, the "environmental footprint" is much less than it might otherwise be. Some of the locations are used for drilling multiple horizontal wells which saves in construction costs for preparing locations and minimizes the cost of moving the rigs.

The top five states based on rig count: Texas 889, Oklahoma 191, North Dakota 174, Louisiana 114 and New Mexico 87. Canada had 154 active rigs working. The most active areas are the Permian Basin and Eagle Ford of Texas and the Williston Basin in North Dakota.

The Texas Railroad Commission reported that March 2014 oil production in Texas was more than 62 million barrels compared to just over 50 million barrels for March 2013. Do the math. At current oil prices, that indicates more than a billion dollar increase just in oil sales within the state compared to one year ago. It appears that many companies are reinvesting the money into more drilling and production projects. It is very interesting, and possibly disturbing, to see the impact that this is having in some areas.

Recent conservations with two separate realtors confirmed that the oil and gas activity is having an impact on their business and that money from the oil areas is going into some land located away from the oil boom area. Who would be surprised that a farmer or rancher with substantial oil income would be interested in buying more land?

From my limited perspective, it is disturbing to see farm and ranch land that is being taken out of production because of the oil and gas activity. If an oil company buys the surface rights to eliminate dealing with a landowner for damages and easements, it may be mutually beneficial for both parties. The operating efficiency of an oil company may be enhanced by being able to place locations, compressors and pipelines in the most cost effective position rather than having to negotiate for every change and addition to a project. In some cases, the surface owner may be able to purchase more productive land in another area away from the oil boom. The net result may be that some land is removed from agriculture production.

Some of the "people impact" may get lost in the details. Like the young man who I met a while back who had worked several years for a fairly large ranching operation that operated a considerable amount of leased acreage. The drilling activity had reached the point that the damage payments and water sales, from wells on the ranch, greatly exceeded the amount received from the grazing lease. A decision was made to end the grazing lease. Consequently, one cowboy's job was eliminated.

In the grand scheme of things it may not sound like very much, but it is probably being played out several times over with a ranch hand here and a farm hand there being relocated. For the residents of small communities in sparsely populated areas, a few people moving out can change the fabric of a community.

There was something about driving into one of the oil boom areas a few months ago that brought up the feeling that "this changes everything". The intensity of the drilling and production activity was such that it must impact everyone in some way. With similar activity occurring in multiple locations across the county, there is no doubt that others are having similar feelings. Sometimes it seems like the only thing that is consistent is that things will change.

A recent trip to one of the towns participating in the oil boom revealed some of the effect on the local economy. I was riding in a vehicle with another consultant and he turned in at a place where the sign was in such poor condition that you couldn't tell what business was located there. It was a restaurant that was packed, early in the evening. The steaks were over twenty dollars and delicious. Times are good. No need to repaint the sign now.

The latest oil price for West Texas Intermediate Crude Oil was just over $99 per barrel. Last week, fed cattle topped $2 a pound on the Merc. Six inches of rain on our place in eastern Runnels county. Green grass is much easier on the eyes than bare pastures. Yes, I sold most of the cows a couple of weeks before the rain started so the check cleared the bank before the rain began. Kept the heifers. Guess that means I'm an optimist! Counting my blessings and giving thanks.

LW58...Oil About Ranching...Read the Document

It seems like the trend to blame technology for sloppy work is increasing with the efforts to blame "cut and paste" for any and all errors in documents. My first big learning experience with cut and paste errors involved some work done by a title company several years ago. Some way a paragraph involving the legal description of a completely unrelated property had been accidentally pasted in the document. It was a reminder that we trust professionals to do their job correctly but realizing that they may see dozens of documents daily where to us "amateurs" the one lease or contract which we may see is the most important to us and could very well be worth our time and effort to read it for ourselves and ask questions.

As most readers are aware, my recommendation is to have a good attorney involved when it comes to leases and contracts. It should be noted that the definition for "good attorney" is left entirely up to the reader.

Recently, a couple of things were brought to my attention that emphasized the need to read and re-read the lease agreement. The excitement of getting into a lease agreement may be focused on "how much are we going to get" and some things of lower priority at the moment may be overlooked. At some point, it may be more important to know how and when a lease terminates. Just like many red-neck stories include something about "where is the back door?" It is a good idea to know where the exits are located when it comes to a lease.

Remember, a lease can last a very long time and may involve several generations. One example is of a unit agreement where it was apparent that one well with very small production held several leases for many years. It would be interesting to know if a clause could have been included about a minimum amount of production over a specific time period. Instead of the single well holding a large amount of lease acreage, would it be possible for portions of the lease, other than designated acreage for that single well, to terminate due to lack of production?

It's just an oil field rumor, which is worth about half a refill from a coffee pot that has been on the burner a little too long. The story relays that a lease had been made with an oil company which proceeded to drill a dry hole on the property. The assumption was made that after the time frame of the lease had expired and that there was no production to hold the lease, that the property owner was free to negotiate a lease with another company. Typically, a lease may be held based on a specific time period and then is held by production for as long as a well is producing on the lease property. The story goes that there was either a "weasel clause" or an omitted clause (maybe cut but not paste) that allowed the company to keep the lease indefinitely once they had drilled to a specified formation. But there was no mention of any production requirement of oil or gas to hold the lease. There may have been no definitive expiration of the lease. What started out as a lease with a time limit to begin drilling operations may not have had the clause about production holding the lease and that the lease would expire at a specified amount of time after production ceases.

It sounds like it is possible that the property owner may have unintentionally double leased the property. We probably won't find out if it really happened that way, but anything that ends with "the lawyers will sort it all out" can make that bitter cup of coffee taste sweet in comparison.

The other one is not an oilfield story but is a reminder to read the documents carefully and ask questions about the details. A tornado did extensive damage to a house to the point that the house was considered a total loss. Unfortunately, it appears that the home owner's insurance coverage had not been upgraded for about twenty years and only covered a small percentage of the replacement cost. Knowing the people involved in this situation makes it a really painful reminder that we need to diligently read all documents and contracts.

This one happened over sixty years ago, before the current cut and paste problems, but could probably happen again. It may have simply been a case of should have turned right instead of left or it may have been an error in a lease description where it was described as the NW quarter instead of the NE quarter. Regardless of the error, a well was drilled on the wrong lease. The person who had the lease for where the well was drilled, reportedly stepped up and paid the other company for the expenses of drilling and casing the well. Whether he had any legal obligation to pay the expenses and whether he would have paid the expenses had it been a dry hole is a question that will never be answered.

Sometimes it is good to have a reminder to read the fine print. I just ordered some new glasses.

LW59...OIL ABOUT RANCHING...WINDMILLS

It was a scene that many western artists have captured. For some reason the windmill about a mile away on the horizon caught my attention. The Canadian River was a couple of miles in the opposite direction. We were in the process of moving in a state of the art drilling rig with the latest mechanical and technological equipment. Driving along a caliche road provided the opportunity to wonder about that windmill and the history behind it.

Was this one of the many homesteads made possible because the mill pumped water for a family or was it the center of a few sections of grazing land that could be used because of the water being pumped for the stock? For how many decades had that windmill been the centerpiece for that piece of the panhandle rangeland? From a historical perspective, the mill may have been important for three generations. How many times across the West did a good water well and sturdy windmill make the difference between success and failure? Now, things were changing rapidly and the drilling for oil and gas would change both the landscape economic conditions to the extent that the windmill might no longer be of importance.

Is it possible that in another two or three generations that the water well marked by that windmill may be even more of a treasure than it was to the original family who celebrated when that well first produced good fresh water? That thought was a reminder of the responsibility that we in the drilling industry to protect the fresh water zones which we drill through in search of oil and gas. The first section of the well is drilled with fresh water (or air in some areas) and protective casing is placed in the ground.

When the casing has been placed at the required depth as required by the appropriate regulatory authority (in Texas it is the Railroad Commission), it is cemented in place. The usual method for cementing the pipe is to pump liquid cement down the pipe and follow the cement with a wiper plug to force the cement through the pipe so that it is pushed outside between the casing and the formation that has been drilled. Having a good cement job around the surface casing performs two important functions. First, it is to protect the water zone and second it is to protect the crew and equipment from the possibility of wellbore fluid or gas coming to surface on the outside of the casing.

After the casing is cemented in place, the blow-out preventers are installed. For the blow-out preventers to be of any use, there must be a good cement seal on the outside of the casing so that the pressure can be contained and handled inside the casing. This is another case of the incentive to do the right thing being much higher than the punishment for doing the wrong thing.

During my first well control school many years ago they showed a picture of a small lake with what appeared to be the crown of a drilling rig sticking up out of the water. The well had broached to surface on the outside of the casing and the water flow had washed out a big hole where the rig was now located. An over pressured formation may have been the cause and the cement job on that casing may or may not have been a factor, but it's a reminder that when we drill a well that we want to do things right for our own protection.

Maybe no one else noticed that particular windmill

near Canadian on that day. Maybe my attention was drawn to it because of memories of being hot and thirsty and riding up to a windmill and being thankful that the wind was blowing just enough so that some water was running out of the pipe and into the reservoir. My horse didn't seem to mind drinking out of the trough, but I appreciated the cool clear water coming right out of the pipe. Getting a drink from a sheep trough many years ago down toward Brackettville one hot day when there was no wind created a real appreciation for enough wind to turn a mill.

    Someday in the future, when the oil and gas wells have been plugged and are only a distant memory, maybe a rider will come up to a windmill that has been maintained and is still pumping cool clear water. Maybe the rider will be thankful for not only the wind but for the oilfield workers who did it right and protected the fresh water zone.

LW60...OIL ABOUT RANCHING...SHEEP

The sheep did seem to be out of place with all of the oil and gas activity on the ranch. Even though there had probably been sheep on the ranch long before there was any motorized vehicle on the ranch. There was something about the way that the sheep moved around in a group, picking out the best grazing spots that gave the impression that they had become strangers in their own home. That was part of what prompted a question from an out of state drilling consultant who is working in the Permian Basin. "Why does this rancher have sheep out here on this ranch when he is surely making a lot more from the oil wells?"

As we continued the discussion, I told him that not having met the rancher, there was no way that I could provide a definite answer. However, I had read a couple of news articles pertaining to the family that told about their ancestors being pioneers and getting their start in ranching by herding sheep. Sheep have probably always been on the ranch. Maybe it's a combination of history and tradition. For several generations, this is what they have done. It's a strong possibility that sheep paid for the ranch.

There are many stories about how sheep paid for more ranches in West Texas than did cattle. That old saying about owning cattle for prestige and sheep to pay the mortgage was probably true for many ranchers. Without the sheep, they might not have ever seen the oil and gas wells. Most readers of this paper do not have to be told about the importance of sheep in our history. Sheep were an important part of my life while growing up, including showing lambs for nine years in 4-H and FFA.

One memorable sheep experience occurred when I was a senior in high school preparing to go to the regional stock show. We were to gather at the Ag barn on Sunday afternoon, one pleasant January day. Being the first one there and a little early, it seemed like a good opportunity to do a little more trimming on a lamb's wool. (This was before lambs were sheared slick to show.) After trimming the lamb and getting it down from the trim table, the lamb slipped away ran across the show ring, hit the fence, broke its neck and ended its show career. There I was alone with a dead lamb. I don't remember if I made a decision or it was just a reaction to drag the lamb out under the calf shed, pick up some loose baling wire, hang the lamb from a rafter and pull out a nice sharp knife and proceed with field dressing the lamb. When the ag teacher drove up, he calmly stated that they were not having a carcass contest, making light of an unfortunate situation but immediately recognizing that I was making the best of a bad situation. In a few minutes time I had an offer from two men who each wanted to purchase a half of the carcass. It was my first experience of "selling on the rail". Part of having sheep is being prepared for the unexpected.

I miss raising sheep and wonder if they will ever re-gain their prominence on ranches and again be a strong economic factor? Will the eight drop shearing rig ever replace the well service unit as the symbol of skilled labor? It's been a long time since the price of wool was a major news item but every day the news reports the current price of oil.

The price of oil has been consistent for quite a while around $100 per barrel. With current events in the Mid-East, it will be interesting to see what happens with the oil market. There seem to be many arguments for it to go either up or down. It seems that many people are wondering why oil is not going down in price with all of the new production coming on line. In this "information age" it would seem everyone would know that our nation is still importing almost 50% of the oil that is consumed.

Visiting with a couple in a hardware store a few weeks ago, the lady commented that she was ready for the "oil glut" to reduce gas prices. To my surprise, she actually thought that we now had an oil surplus and prices should go down at any time. She didn't have a clue that the U.S. is still importing nearly as much oil as is being produced domestically.

Production is continuing to increase in several areas. Congratulations to North Dakota for crossing the threshold of producing one million barrels per day. Recently there were some news reports about that event. It would be interesting to make a trip to North Dakota and see what is going on there. Several years ago I spent some time there at an oil field called "Big Stick" so named after Teddy Roosevelt and his famous admonition to "Walk softly and carry a big stick." One report mentioned that 70% of the oil in North Dakota is being shipped by rail. Seems to be a shortage of pipelines. The "rumor" a couple of years ago about oil being shipped by rail from Barnhart turned out to be more than just a rumor but I haven't seen any reports on how much oil is going through San Angelo on that rail line. It's been a long time since lambs were loaded out in that same area and shipped to market on those rails.

The green landscape is nice to see whether at home or at a well site looking across the pasture. Some sheep could sure turn those weeds into some healthy lean meat. Just wondering how much trouble that a high school kid would get into today for butchering a lamb at the show barn. The sharp knife alone would probably result in a suspension. Times change. Now they don't even let grown men carry pocket knives in the oilfield. You can let me know how you are enjoying the oil boom (or not).

LW61...OIL ABOUT RANCHING...FOOTPRINT & RECYCLING

"Reducing the footprint" is a phrase typically used to emphasize environmental awareness and political correctness. As you drive through, or fly over, an area that is busy with oilfield activity and see the many roads and locations, it appears that there must be no concern for "reducing the footprint". The biggest reason for an oil company to reduce the footprint is when it will reduce costs. One of the benefits of horizontal drilling is that multiple wells may be drilled from one location. This reduces construction costs for multiple pads and reserve pits, reduces rig moving expense when the next well is on the same location and may facilitate the concentration of production facilities. A reduced footprint has been made possible through modern technology.

An article in the Midland Reporter-Telegram told about a company that claims to have water treatment technology to remove the salt from oilfield produced water and turn it into good fresh water suitable for human consumption. It will be interesting to see if this turns out to be the formula for which many have been searching for a long time. No specifics were given about the capital and operational costs other than something about being economical. Water economics is highly subjective, as was exemplified many years ago when bottled water was just beginning to be a popular item in convenience stores. A cowboy/cotton farmer (nicknamed Rawhide) who also owns a fresh water station somewhere in the Permian Basin, purchased a bottle of water for something like seventy-cents. While driving down the road he commented that he was on the wrong side of the water business since he was selling water for ten cents a barrel (yes, it was long time ago) and buying it for seventy cents a pint. There can be significant differences in how "economically feasible" may be defined. Hopefully, this new water treatment system or something similar will turn out to be economically feasible because there's considerable need for it from the Pecos River to the Salt Fork of the Brazos.

We don't have to look very far to be reminded of the need for water. Recently, on an oil field lease, there were two quail walking away from an old cement water trough. A closer look revealed that there was no water in the trough and it appeared that it had been abandoned for a few years. With the oil and gas production and several years of drought, livestock production was probably no longer of importance and the windmill and trough had been neglected. It made me wonder what the quail were thinking as they walked away from that empty trough. Since quail may be worth more than cattle, there may be some incentive to maintain some of those abandoned windmills.

It's no secret that the oil drilling and fracking operations use a large volume of water but some claim that it's only a small percentage compared to the domestic and irrigation consumption. However, the need for water continues to grow with more activity in the oilfield. The Hughes Rig count reports that there were 1,873 drilling rigs working in the U.S. as of June 27, 2014. This number is up 15 from the previous week and up 125 from one year ago. The Texas Railroad Commission reports that Texas produced just over ten percent more oil during the first four months of 2014 compared to the previous year. Another news report indicated that Texas was now producing more oil than the #2 Opec country. Who would have picked Texas on that bet twenty years ago?

More economic good news comes from the natural gas industry. There have been reports about some Liquified Natural Gas facilities that were designed and built for importing LNG. With the long lead time required to construct these facilities, enough gas wells were drilled to not only eliminate the need for importing LNG but now there is enough gas that facilities that were designed for importing will now be used for exports. Reversing that check valve in the cash flow line must have a significant impact on the Texas economy.

Maybe this oil boom has hit a new psychological phase and we're accepting it as the new normal. Not as many questions are asked now about how long will this boom last. Early in the boom, when the young guys were buying fancy new pick-ups some of us wondered, and hoped, that the boom would last long enough for them to make all the payments. Now, some of the older guys (even older than me) are buying new pick-ups, probably so that they can ride off into the sunset. Instead of making payments they probably follow the admonition of the old gentleman who told his grandson that of all the options available on a new pick-up that the only two things needed on a pick-up are a trailer hitch and a clear title.

LW62...OIL ABOUT RANCHING...JULY 4...FREEDOM... PILOT DON ORR

July 4, somewhere in the Permian Basin. One more holiday in the oilfield with no record of how many this makes. Some records are better not kept. It's a good time to remember that it is Independence Day and think of our freedom. Rules and regulations are often counterproductive and at times almost overwhelming. The decision to be involved in the oil business or farming and ranching is still a choice that we make..... although at times it may seem that it chose us rather than us choosing it.

A property owner may have an opportunity to negotiate an oil and gas lease. This is not something that is forced upon the property owner by the industry or by the government. The government regulations and taxes come later. A private property owner has the freedom to make the choice about whether to lease the property. Whether the decision is because they don't want to put up with the activity and property damage or if they are greedy and simply want more money than is being offered, the owner has freedom to make the decision.

If a rancher wants to turn out some big boned bulls in March so that he can be calving heifers in the snow at Christmas, that decision is left up to the rancher. Choices have consequences. Freedom is like prosperity; too much of either may be hazardous. We have the freedom to choose the type and breed of animals that we want. Calves can be sold at weaning, pre-conditioned or kept on retained ownership through the feedlot. The sale may be through an auction, by private treaty or on the rail. The rancher has freedom to choose.

An oil company has the freedom to obtain leases and then freedom to drill on acquired leases. Nobody forces anyone to be in the business of drilling wells. They may have to drill by a certain date to meet a deadline or lose the lease but that deadline is the result of a choice made by the company. An oil company is not forced to be in that business. Like the rancher, they have the freedom to choose.

It is very interesting to see that the three big oil booms currently in progress, Bakken Shale, Permian Basin and Eagle Ford, primarily involve private property. Numerous owners and companies are involved by way of their own free will to participate. Free enterprise is not free, but we have the freedom to participate.

There is also the freedom to disperse controversial and even incorrect information. When the Alaska pipeline was proposed over thirty years ago, there were some groups complaining that the pipeline would be destructive to wildlife. Several reports have come out since the construction indicating that the pipeline improved the habitat and has been beneficial for wildlife.

A major construction project has been shut down due to lack of approval for a pipeline originating in Canada to transport crude oil to refineries in Oklahoma and Texas. There are "concerns" about oil spills. All kinds of so called special interest groups have the freedom to be "concerned" as well as the freedom to raise money for their "cause". Unlike the rancher who makes the bad choice when selecting bulls for heifers or the oil company that misses the zone and drills a dry hole, some special interest groups seem to be free from any consequences of their actions.

With all of the fear mongering about the possibility of an oil spill from a pipeline, the question of probability seems to be ignored. Here's a history question: If you live between Austin and Albuquerque, name the location, year and volume of the worst oil spill in that area from a pipeline in the past 100 years. If no event comes to mind, maybe that's a sign that the pipeline companies are doing a good job because they have a vested interest in preventing spills. Today's technology gives more advantages to operate remote valves to reduce the volume of a spill. A leak is not profitable. No company wants money to be running out on the ground.

Freedom to participate and compete in the oil and gas drilling industry is exemplified by the many of the support and service companies that operate as independent contractors. With no central planning or government intervention, the free market system is providing the necessary goods, supplies and personnel to keep all of these drilling rigs running twenty-four hours a day with only limited disruption. There is the freedom to participate along with the freedom to fail. At least we have a choice. Thank God we're free. Even free to work on a holiday. It's a choice.

Sometimes we are reminded that freedom is not free and did not come easy. The phone call was to inform us that one of our WW2 heroes passed on July 5 at age 92. Don Orr was a fighter pilot and flew 200 missions, reported to be the second highest number of any pilot in WW2. After 100 missions, pilots had the option to get out but he stayed because the job was not finished. After the war, Don and his wife Vi spent 34 years as missionaries in Colombia.

LW63...Oil About Ranching...Price Dropping...Snowmobile

A dozen vehicles being fueled a few minutes before 6AM on a Friday morning at Sterling City are proof that the oil boom is still going strong. It made me wonder how many horses, if any, were being saddled in the county at the same time. Just the thought proves that some of us never adjust to all the changes.

The third headline proclaiming that oil prices are dropping caught my attention. One prediction was that oil would be cheaper in the fourth quarter. Further reading revealed that the falling prices had recently dropped seven percent. Seven percent is more shrink than would be acceptable on a set of steers, will affect cash flow from producing wells but it is probably not enough of a drop to cause immediate panic in the oil field. The story predicting lower prices in the fourth quarter finished with a prediction that oil would average around $100 per barrel. Having been through two major price drops where the price dropped by seventy percent, a seven percent drop does not create a crisis but can create a sense of nervousness about like seeing the sun break through the clouds after three rainy days and wondering if it is the beginning of another dry spell. (Thanks to Elmer Kelton for that memory.)

The prediction of $100 per barrel average for oil in the fourth quarter sounds more like a prediction of stability since oil has been in that range for quite a while. There are several arguments being made for both oil and cattle that we are now in new economic paradigm and that the old rules and past experiences no longer apply. Evidence supporting those arguments happen to be all around us. A decreasing supply of cattle combined with an increasing population is creating a seller's market for beef. Crowded restaurants further support this theory. It appears that many customers have adjusted to the higher prices as evidenced by the reaction to a table for four having prime rib (small cut) and being surprised that the cost was less than twenty dollars per person, while being served on white table cloths in a restaurant with an incredible view. Everyone at the table could remember eating for a week on twenty dollars back in college days.

Gas prices are another area where the customers appear to have adjusted to higher prices. Many thought that the customers would not adjust to gasoline above two dollars per gallon. Now there are traffic problems all around us caused by people burning $3.50 per gallon gasoline. Not saying that they like it and that nobody is complaining about it, but people are buying it. Some people are making adjustments like one young man who traded his pickup for an economy car that has been averaging thirty-nine miles per gallon.

With increasing domestic oil production, the questions continue: When will the increase of supply result in lower prices? Recently, this country reached the production achievement of producing just over 50% of the oil that is being consumed. Right now, it appears that the demand for fuel, very similar to beef, is matching or exceeding the supply. Anytime, that the term "new economics" is used in an explanation about supply and demand, it is a reminder that human nature has not changed and that getting comfortable with selling at high markets is a sign to be alert.

For as long as I can remember, it's been a tradition of this publication to run a picture of a snow scene on the front page along about mid-summer. That may have something to do with how I respond to questions about how I'm liking the heat. At those times, it brings to mind about some of the cold times while working rigs in Wyoming. The coldest temperature that I ever witnessed was 42 degrees below zero, actual temp with no wind chill adjustment. The closest call that I ever had in a weather related incident was taking a ride on a snow mobile. Full disclosure – I didn't know what I was doing and I broke the rule of going alone. While riding over the snowy mountains at 8,000' elevation, the scenery was fabulous. The decision to take a closer look at some trees was not a good one. At the edge of the clearing, just after crossing the shadow line of the trees, the consistency of the snow changed. Out in the open where it had been exposed to sunlight there was a nice crust on top. In the shadows the snow was powder and the machine dropped about four feet and was stuck. After struggling with the machine for a while, it became alarming that sweating at those temperatures and conditions was not good. The only way to get away from the snowmobile was to crawl through the snow and work my way to the area with a good crust on surface and then follow the tracks out.

  The next day, it was necessary to walk back to the snowmobile. It took a while to walk around and tromp down the snow to start a path way to make a run out of the powder. If it had not been for the knowledge and experience of loading mutton lambs on a double decker, I would not have known how to tail that machine up onto the crusty snow. Then it was an uneventful ride back to the camp at the rig site. That was more than thirty years ago and I haven't ridden a snowmobile since. It's another oil field story that is better told while sitting in the shade, drinking lemonade and complaining about the heat than going through the experience again. For a few moments, the memory of nearly freezing makes the summer heat seem a little bit more tolerable.

LW66...OIL ABOUT RANCHING...TRASH

As a critic of the current tax system and long time supporter of the FairTax or some other form of flat tax, it is only the never say never philosophy that has prevented taking a stand for never supporting any new tax of any kind. With all of the big items that landowners and oil companies deal with at various times, there is a little item that is causing great consternation, catching nearly everybody's attention and seems to be getting worse instead of better. The culprit is the proliferation of the lightweight, functional and convenient little plastic bags used by almost every retail establishment.

In many ways it is difficult to not like the little bags that are masterpieces of design with a very respectable strength to weight ratio. They come on rolls or in boxes by the thousands. Consumers seem to have a great love affair for the little plastic bags which seem to do an effective job up to a point. But how does the little bag identify pickles in a glass jar and split so that the jar crashes onto the concrete garage floor as opposed to the soft rug just inside the back door?

In spite of their weak points, the little bags have some incredible qualities that belie their simple appearance. Consider the aerodynamic, navigational and tethering qualities of the little boogers. A bag can be rolled up and stuck in the door pocket of a pick-up and it will crawl out, unroll and take flight. It does not land in one of the openings at the bottom of a brush pile or in a badger hole. No, it seeks out a target that is waiting to be a flagpole and attaches itself tighter than a bow-line knot wrapped in gray tape. It flaps around for everyone to see. After the best spots are taken, other bags will settle for snagging onto the barbed wire fence, top row, or some kind of sticker bush in such a way that it will be visible from "this side" in such a way that three bags transform a landowner's mind into believing that there is TRASH ALL OVER THE RANCH.

It is probably safe to say that a significant percentage of these loose bags are unintentional littering. It's a problem for which nobody wants to take ownership and roughnecks are all in the "not mine" crowd and really don't like to be on clean up detail to go out and pick up somebody else's trash that is scattered around the location. A crew would rather clean out a mud pit than go pick the little bags out of the bushes and off the fence.

The really serious issue with the plastic bags blowing across the pasture is when livestock eat one of the bags. This may cause any number of complications that may result in a fatality. Through the years there have been various reports of livestock deaths from ingesting plastic bags. Plastic bags blowing across a pasture are a serious matter for livestock owners.

An unscientific observation indicates that the litter problem with the plastic bags is getting worse instead of better. There was some talk a while back about the possibility of a city voting for either a tax or to outlaw the bags. It would be an interesting economic study of human behavior to determine what level of taxation would be the death knell for the plastic bags. Would consumers balk at ten cents per bag or would it take two dollars? It might set a bench mark for "death by taxes". Any new tax is difficult to swallow but that may be preferable to having a cow swallow the bag. If the big city liberals, who buy their meat at the store rather than killing animals after they buy their gas at the station rather than drilling in their backyard, are the group that eliminates the plastic bag litter problem, it may be a historic political moment when several traditionally opposing groups agree on an issue.

Oil companies spend a lot of money handling trash. In the old days, a pit was dug and the mud sacks and other paper trash would be burned in the pit or covered to decompose. Now, it is not acceptable to pollute the air by burning the trash on location. A trailer is rented to collect the trash so that it can be hauled away by a vehicle which is polluting the air over several miles. This seems to be a much more acceptable form of pollution. Observation has revealed that there is no such thing as diminishing returns regarding the amount of undesignated pollution that is acceptable; provided that it occurs while preventing some designated pollution.

You do the best you can, pay the price and believe the problem has been handled and then learn of the weak link in the chain of events. Fortunately, this was related by a mud engineer and not personal experience. The mud man decided to dispose of some magazines and other trash that had accumulated in his pick-up. The trash trailer on location was the ideal and proper receptacle for trash. A few days later, he received a call from a mad landowner accusing him of dumping trash on his ranch. Apparently, someone working for the trash trailer company decided to save time by dumping a load in a remote area and the only "trace" was the trash with the mud engineer's information. One bad player makes the entire system look bad, even if it's a one in a million occurrence. Another benefit of identity theft prevention is that it can also prevent identity.

LW67...OIL ABOUT RANCHING...CATTLE AND OIL

How about these cattle prices? A friend sent a note that he trailer weaned and sold a heifer calf weighing 765 pounds for $1.80 per pound for a total of $1377.00. The prediction for $2500 pairs was filled and did not establish a ceiling with reports of some now bringing much more. Oil is staying strong with West Texas Intermediate closing above $97 on August 15. There have not been any major price swings for crude oil recently but some fluctuation blamed on the crisis in Ukraine and in the Mid-East. Analysts and economists in both camps are now claiming that the markets are in a new paradigm and that many of the fundamentals have changed. Maybe it's just going to get better and better. Let the good times roll! For all of us who wished for one more oil boom and for weaning calves to bring a thousand bucks a head, we've seen some dreams come true and have a lot for which to be thankful.

An individual who lives a couple of states to the North told me that he had quit eating beef because it was too high and that he was going straight chicken. He went on to say that he believed that beef was so high because "they" have created an artificial shortage of beef to raise prices just like "they" created the artificial oil shortage in the mid '70's to raise gas prices. No point in arguing with someone who does not want to be confused with the facts but it was interesting to listen to him and realize that he truly believed that the high markets were caused by and are a result of manipulation rather than supply and demand in a free market.

With cow numbers being the lowest that they've been in about sixty years or so and with the population having doubled or tripled it is difficult to accept that the beef shortage is a contrived occurrence. Those in the beef industry are aware of feedlots and packing plants that have closed due to the decrease in numbers. Occasionally a headline will appear including something about an "oil glut" due to the increased production but fails to mention that until recently the U.S. was importing more than 50% of the oil that was consumed in this country.

When oil production increased to the point that domestic production exceeded 50% of consumption, it was an opportunity for celebration of some great accomplishments of ingenuity and innovation. Apparently, very few people even noticed that the stats changed. The study of supply and demand is a very interesting activity. Getting a grasp of the term "elasticity of supply and demand" was not easy because the targets are continually moving. Some recent observations indicate that the demand for gasoline is very high and that consumers seemed to be accepting the price because few if any bicycles were seen on the highway. Waiting in line at a couple of restaurants on the same trip was evidence that consumers are accepting the prices there too. At least they (we) are able to complain about the high prices with a mouth full.

This is not to diminish that some people are being hurt by the higher prices of food and energy but just an observation that there is not a huge rejection from consumers regarding the higher prices. Admittedly, working in the oilfield gives me a twisted view of the prices of some things. Justification of prices is made easier by the fact now the small prime rib or filet is more than adequate and a few dollars cheaper. A trip is more likely to be avoided because it would result in a long late trip home rather than the price of fuel.

At some point the increasing production of oil in the U.S. may result in lower prices or some technology may impact the fundamentals. A check on the Texas Railroad Commission website shows that permits are up so far this year and that completions at this point in 2014 are up more than 20% compared to a year ago. Turning the cow numbers around may be a more difficult proposition. Maybe some of the people with a lot of oil production will invest in heifers and rebuild the cow herd. Of course, the question comes up as to why somebody living the Psalm 23:5 dream would want to invest in cows. This can be answered by the fact that some people are addicted to the cow business and just can't help it. One man did tell me that his oil checks were such that the price of cows did not matter because if he wanted them he could buy them. For many of us who still have some scarred memory of the cattle wreck in the 70's, it might be good for us to remember that the government stepped in to put price controls on beef. They had already done the same for oil several years earlier. Maybe we can enjoy riding the crest of the wave a little longer before the bureaucrats come to help us. One friend keeps reminding me that he and I are a lot closer to the finish line than the starting line and that we just need to enjoy it while we can, even though it's with an oily hat and not near enough cattle.

LW68...Oil About Ranching...Prices Aug. 2014

West Texas Intermediate Crude Oil was selling for $98.09 on August 11, then $96.44 on Aug. 18 and the posted price on Aug. 24 was $92.50. One year ago, oil was selling for a little over $107 per barrel. A thirteen percent drop in price in one year is enough to capture some attention. A check of oil futures showed the October contract closing recently at $93.65. There are some reports that the increased oil production has filled the pipelines and that some oil is now being discounted substantially. The problem appears to be that there is a lack of pipeline capacity for moving the oil to the refineries. The U.S. is still importing a tremendous amount of oil. Those ocean tankers that haul foreign oil just can't get to West Texas to pick up a load.

Many events are going on all over the world that may affect the price of oil. Too many variables make it difficult for the experts to make accurate predictions about prices. One headline made the claim that Oil is the new Gold Standard. Several good arguments can probably be made to support that claim since most businesses are affected by energy prices. A slight downward trend and a pipeline transportation overload can be changed quickly by any number of events. Some of us keep looking over our shoulder.

Meanwhile, the oil boom continues and some areas of the Permian Basin look as though whole counties are turning into one continuous drilling location. It doesn't look like the old pictures of Spindletop and Kilgore but there are many rigs at work and rumors that more may be moving in. Every day, somewhere, a rancher is probably having his first experience with oilfield activity on his property.

One reader wrote about a problem with thread protectors left on location and a calf stepping into one of the protectors. Those things go on a lot easier than they come off. A thread protector is a small cap that is placed on the end of the pipe to protect the threads when the pipe is being hauled and handled. The thread protectors must be removed before the pipe can be used. It was mentioned that the relatives who share in the oil royalties are never around to help with something like roping a calf to get a thread protector off its hoof with a mad cow in hot pursuit. But the resident cowboy seems to be expected to explain why the oil check was lower last month or when the next well will be drilled.

It seemed that the worst case scenario for thread protectors was when a calf or cow stepped in one that was tight and worked into a position where it hindered movement and cut through the skin just above the hoof line to cause an infection. When the foot and ankle swells, the protector is not easy to remove. If it is metal, it may take a hacksaw or some tedious work with hand held grinder. A plastic one may not be much easier to remove.

It has long been observed that the less that a cow knows about a particular object, the more likely it is that she will chew on it. One cow had a silly look on her face and was holding her head just a little different. At a distance it was difficult to see what might be wrong. Closer observation revealed that she had attempted to eat a four and a half inch thread protector. It was one of those open ended ones that is just a hard plastic ring. Somehow she had worked it around so that it went around her chin and over her teeth. For those of you who have ever been bitten by a cow, you know the teeth structure on the lower jaw. Somehow, she had gotten this chin ring in place just behind her teeth and it was as secure as if it had been designed to snap in place. There was no way that it was coming off without some help. The cow probably couldn't drink and definitely could not have eaten with that thing in her mouth. That protector had probably been left behind when a well was drilled ten or twenty years prior.

It seems that the one who makes the discovery is the one who must handle the problem. Several years ago, a pile of metal protectors was found on a place where we ran some cattle. To prevent a problem with a calf stepping through a protector, the decision was made to gather and deliver the protectors to the local ag teacher for students to use for welding practice. Sometimes we just have to clean up the mess behind whoever left it.

Even though we are doing a better job of handling trash and junk in the oilfield, inevitably there will be mistakes and misdeeds. After the oil boom is over and all of the big equipment is gone, there will be some cowboy who has the misfortune finding a thread protector on a calf's ankle. Hopefully he will be young and agile enough to handle it. If not, maybe it will be the day before deer season when all the relatives show up ready to go hunting and he'll have all the help he needs. Sure. To quote the late C.R. Pinkerton, "Blessed is he who expecteth nothing, for he shall not be disappointed."

LW70...OIL ABOUT RANCHING...ROYALTY OWNERSHIP

West Texas Intermediate Crude Oil was reported at $89.75 per barrel early on 9-8-2014. It is not clear whether the drop is due more to world markets or to regional pipelines and railroads not being able to handle all of the increased production. The price drop will affect corporate profits, cash flow and royalty payments.

One reader commented that royalty ownership is probably the simplest and best way to be involved in the oil business. A royalty owner who does not own any of the surface does not have to deal with damages and disruptions. A royalty owner may live far away and not even be aware of the traffic and work activity. They sure have it much easier than the roustabouts, roughnecks and the many other workers who have to deal with everything from the weather to unrealistic deadlines and weeks away from home.

The highest risk for a royalty owner may be from getting a paper cut from opening the envelope when the check arrives. Even mailbox money comes with some amount of risk. With most companies now doing on line deposits, even the possibility of paper cuts can be eliminated.

According to one group representing Texas royalty owners, in 2013 more than eleven and one-half billion (yes, billion) dollars was paid out to 570,000 families for an average of just over twenty thousand dollars per family for the year. It was not clear whether the term family also included institutional and corporate ownership. If the numbers are correct, that is evidence that the majority of owners are not receiving millions and for every royalty owner who receives a million dollars there are many receiving much less than the twenty thousand average.

A suggestion was received about doing a comparison of mineral and royalty ownership in the United States and how it compares to that of other nations. That appeared to be an overwhelming task for someone who is not being adequately funded through some research grant. Just a little checking did indicate that the United States may be the only country that has substantial mineral and royalty ownership by private individuals. This tied in with a somewhat related study that was an eye opener about economics and private property ownership.

It may have been an unintended consequence. After studying agriculture economics, it seemed clear to me that a nations economy was almost totally dependent upon their natural resources. Most of which contributed to the essentials of producing food, fuel, fiber and housing. The study of economics has been somewhat of a lifetime pursuit. Being production oriented, that is always thinking about things like pounds of gain per day and barrels produced per day, it was only natural to continue to think about economics from a natural resources basis.

The questions went something like this: "What are the two most important components of a strong economy? What do the strongest economies in the world have in common?" My mind raced with trying to pick out the top two natural resources among food, fuel, gold, trade route accessibility, national defense and a few others. The list grew so long that is seemed impossible to pick only two but the country boy experience was leaning heavily toward food and water.

The answer was a real eye opener. #1 is Private Property ownership and #2 is the Rule of Law. Those even ranked higher than a democratic form of government. Rather than dispel my beliefs regarding the importance of natural resources for a strong economy, those two rules laid out the foundation and mechanism for developing and distributing (or growing and marketing) of the natural resources. It was a reminder of the concept "it's not what you've got but what you do with what you've got that matters".

Mineral interests and royalties seem to have some mystical or abstract qualities. Unlike the surface of the ground, the underlying minerals cannot be readily seen or touched. In many instances, the mineral interest beneath the surface was merely incidental to the surface ownership which was originally homesteaded for agricultural production. It is my understanding that in Texas law, the mineral interest/ownership takes precedent over the surface ownership. It would be interesting to learn WHY the law was established that the mineral interest takes precedent over surface. The important thing to know is that it does take precedence and the ongoing basis for that is the rule of law. Many people in sub-divisions in the Barnett Shale area were sorely disappointed to discover that somebody else literally owned what was under their house.

All of that just to point out that minerals and royalties can be private property. It can be compared to other private property such as stocks, bonds, commercial property, or other private investments. Just like other private property, the buying, selling and exploitation of mineral interests is dependent upon "the rule of law". Mineral interest ownership varies greatly among the states. It is interesting to see the difference when the ownership is private individuals as compared to state and federal lands. For a real education, go to your County Appraisal Office and ask them to explain the process for valuation and taxing of oil and gas mineral interests.

LW72...Oil About Ranching...Drive By Questions

West Texas Intermediate Crude was posted at $92.86 per barrel on September 15, 2014 at the terminal in Cushing, Oklahoma. Cow prices are so high that it can be embarrassing when friends and neighbors are witness to a purchase at such prices.

An interesting question came from a reader who is curious about some oilfield activity in his area. A drilling rig had spent some time on a location and then was moved off. Later a pumping unit and tank battery were put in place and it appeared to be a producing well. Some time later, a workover rig was on the location and then later the original drilling rig came back and the pump jack was moved away. Then the drilling rig was moved away and some frac tanks and equipment were on the location. The question: What is going on?

Now I know how a veterinarian feels when someone is trying to get him to diagnose a rare combination of symptoms-----over the phone. Actually, it's a good question and there are several possibilities to consider. Just knowing some of the possibilities may help to understand some of the potential risk and operational headaches that may occur in drilling a well and trying to get it to produce.

It's a high probability that everything is not going according to plan and that some problem has been encountered down hole. The well may not have been drilled to the proper depth. On a well that is ten thousand feet deep, more than 300 joints of drill pipe and other components will be run in the hole. With a couple of bit trips and other activity, it is possible for an error in measurement or joint count. It shouldn't happen with today's duplication of records with all the high tech equipment, but it can. There's a reason that we count before we start drilling and compare that with the final depth of the well. With all the high tech stuff we do, it's still the fundamentals that matter. If the well is not drilled to the right zone, it won't produce.

It's possible that it was drilled to the correct zone but there may have been a problem with the casing. Maybe the casing was of insufficient strength and collapsed. Possibly the threads were not machined properly and there was a failure under pressure. Maybe the cement job was inadequate and there was inadequate coverage to seal the area between the casing and productive zone. This could result in an "uncontrolled environment" resulting in the desired zone not being isolated.

It is possible that human error, equipment failure and/or just something unimagined (we ain't never seen anything like this before*) in the formation caused problems.

Even though we don't know what happened, it is probable that something is not right and that instead of a well making everybody rich, it has become a money pit requiring remedial work. The workover rig may have been making an attempt to drill deeper with "slim hole tools" inside the casing to get the well to the desired depth. Or, if there was a casing or cement failure they may have been trying to sort of put a patch on the problem. Sometimes, Murphy's Law kicks in and it is all of the above. After exhausting all ideas and running over budget that well may have been plugged. A total waste. It's a lot like when the cow dies just after running up a vet and medicine bill exceeding the original healthy value.

With the drilling rig coming back to the location, it may have been a case of drilling a new well just a short distance from the original abandoned well. If that is the case, the investment for a well on that location has been more than doubled. It doesn't take a math wiz to get an idea what that might do to cash flow and return on investment. Right now, it looks like the oil industry is a high profit enterprise, but it also remains a very high risk endeavor. It's a reminder that getting oil out of the ground is not simple, not easy and never a sure thing. It takes a lot of effort from people on the scene and behind the scene. One reader who had some oilfield experience a few decades ago said that he believed that oil was not overpriced when all of the risk and efforts are taken into consideration. The market appears to agree with him.

Hopefully, the equipment that is now on location is an indication that the well has been drilled to a productive zone. The "frac tanks" aren't always used for frac purposes. Best case scenario is that the well is flowing oil and they had to bring in some portable frac tanks to hold the oil.

(*common oilfield saying)

LW73...OIL ABOUT RANCHING...HUNTING SAFETY

Hunting leases have probably increased in value right along with the price of oil and the related effect that the oil boom has had on the economy. Oil people, along with being some of the rancher's best customers for beef, are a formidable presence at many hunting camps. Many of us are going into fall in the best conditions that we've seen in many years. The early cool dampness early in the mornings can make a person look forward to hunting season.

Some oilfield people want a hunting lease that is far from the oilfield so that they can see different landscapes and not see any reminders of the work that they are trying to get away from for a short time. Then there are other groups of city hunters who have a hunting lease where there is oil & gas activity on the ranch. In the interest of safety, there are several things that need to be considered. The statistics won't give us credit for the life that might be saved by making someone aware of these hazards.

Don't just warn the hunters about oilfield equipment in the area but SCARE them into staying away from it. It might be advisable to put something in writing as part of the lease and maybe post it in the hunting camp. Emphasize that the oil field locations, facilities and pipelines are merely adjacent to and not part of the hunting lease and should be treated as a separate entity. Those areas are probably a separate private property due to the lease and easement agreements between the landowner and oil operator. Entering into or making contact with any of that equipment may be trespassing.

A tank battery with an inviting stairway is more than just a mere temptation for someone who recognizes that it would be a good look out point. Maybe if you tell them that it is dangerous and that it is also illegal because it constitutes trespassing, you can get the point across that they do not touch or enter and maybe only look at it with fear and trembling. Based on personal experience, I do not know what it would take to keep a small boy on a pony away from something that was in "his pasture". Many of the close calls that I survived were not even known that the activity was a close call until twenty years after the fact when a situation was presented in an oilfield safety meeting. Those who fall into this same category realize that it's a miracle that any of us survived.

As a small boy, I don't know whether I was warned and if so whether it was understood that this was directed to me rather than some hypothetical situation and that it also applied to not only that day but every day. Little boys have minds that work in mysterious ways when they work, but sometimes are just turned off. Keep children away.

A tank with oil in it also has gas fumes that are highly explosive. A hunter who uses a tank battery for a lookout point and cannot resist "the best shot in years" may fire (fire being the operative word) his last shot, near that gas vent line or leaking hatch. Just as hazardous is the potential for poison gas. If there are "Poison Gas" warning signs on the ranch, it needs to be clearly understood regarding the potential for danger. If the potential levels are high, it might be recommended to lease the hunting only to people who work in the oilfield and understand the warning signs and the potential danger. Make sure they have a current H2S Safety Card and sign off accepting all responsibility and liability.

A pumping unit may be just as tempting for a lookout since most have a ladder up the side. For those unaware, that ladder may be an invitation to disaster. Most pumping units are electric powered and start without warning. Those ladders are usually located in close proximity to the counter-weights which travel in a circular motion. Being in the wrong place when the pumping unit starts probably won't be just a close call. When that much steel is involved, the laws of physics are unforgiving.

If hunters see a leak in a pipeline, they need to know what numbers to call to report the leak. The rancher may be the first call but there also needs to be an emergency number to alert the company. If the leak is a gas leak, everyone must stay upwind and on higher ground. Stay away and don't drive through an area where gas may be leaking.

People do work and live safely in areas where oil field equipment is located. By understanding the risks and maintaining proper distances, the degree of danger may be significantly reduced. Warn those who will heed the warning and scare everyone who doesn't.

Be sure and check with your attorney and insurance agent regarding risk, liability and appropriate documentation. You could nail this column to the wall of the hunting lodge. Better yet, put in the lease that all hunters are required to have their own subscription to the Livestock Weekly. Here's hoping that everyone has a wonderful and safe hunting season.

LW74...OIL ABOUT RANCHING...FRACKING RESEARCH REPORT

The Department of Energy released a report on research of hydraulic fracturing in the oil field, titled: "An Evaluation of Fracture Growth andGas/Fluid Migration as Horizontal Marcellus Shale Gas Wells are Hydraulically Fractured in Greene County, Pennsylvania."

Quotes and data are from the following link: http://www.netl.doe.gov/File%20Library/Research/onsite%20research/publications/NETL-TRS-3-2014_Greene-County-Site_20140915_1_1.pdf.

It's worth going to the site just to read the lengthy disclaimer.

This is the most in depth and comprehensive report (about thirty pages) that I've seen about whether oil field hydraulic fracturing is damaging other zones. Their summary, in its entirety, is included below. Please pay special attention to the conclusion.

EXECUTIVE SUMMARY

This field study monitored the induced fracturing of six horizontal Marcellus Shale gas wells in Greene County, Pennsylvania. The study had two research objectives: 1) to determine the maximum height of fractures created by hydraulic fracturing at this location; and 2) to determine if natural gas or fluids from the hydraulically fractured Marcellus Shale had migrated 3,800 ft upward to an overlying Upper Devonian/Lower Mississippian gas field during or after hydraulic fracturing.

The Tully Limestone occurs about 280 ft above the

Marcellus Shale at this location and is considered to be a barrier to upward fracture growth when intact. Microseismic monitoring using vertical geophone arrays located 10,288 microseismic events during hydraulic fracturing; about 40% of the events were above the Tully Limestone, but all events were at least 2,000 ft below producing zones in the overlying Upper Devonian/Lower Mississippian gas field, and more than 5,000 ft below drinking water aquifers.

Monitoring for evidence of fluid and gas migration was performed during and after the hydraulic fracturing of six horizontal Marcellus Shale gas wells. This monitoring program included: 1) gas pressure and production histories of three Upper Devonian/Lower Mississippian wells; 2) chemical and isotopic analysis of the gas produced from seven Upper Devonian/Lower Mississippian wells; 3) chemical and isotopic analysis of water produced from five Upper Devonian/Lower Mississippian wells; and 4) monitoring for perfluorocarbon tracers in gas produced from two Upper Devonian/Lower Mississippian wells.

Gas production and pressure histories from three Upper Devonian/Lower Mississippian gas wells that directly overlie stimulated, horizontal Marcellus Shale gas wells recorded no production or pressure increase in the 12-month period after hydraulic fracturing. An increase would imply communication with the over-pressured Marcellus Formation below.

Sampling to detect possible migration of fluid and gas from the underlying hydraulicallyfractured Marcellus Shale gas wells commenced 2 months prior to hydraulic fracturing to establish background conditions. Analyses have been completed for gas samples collected up to 8 months after hydraulic fracturing and for produced water samples collected up to 5 months after hydraulic fracturing. Samples of gas and produced water continue to be collected monthly (produced water) and bimonthly (gas) from seven Upper Devonian/Lower Mississippian gas wells.

Current findings are: 1) no evidence of gas migration from the Marcellus Shale; and 2) no evidence of brine migration from the Marcellus Shale.

Four perfluorocarbon tracers were injected with hydraulic fracturing fluids into 10 stages of a 14-stage, horizontal Marcellus Shale gas well during stimulation. Gas samples collected from two Upper Devonian/Lower Mississippian wells that directly overlie the tracer injection well were analyzed for presence of the tracer. No tracer was found in 17 gas samples taken from each of the two wells during the 2-month period after completion of the hydraulic fracturing.

An Evaluation of Fracture Growth and Gas/Fluid Migration as Horizontal Marcellus Shale Gas Wells are Hydraulically Fractured in Greene County, Pennsylvania.

Conclusions of this study are: 1) the impact of hydraulic fracturing on the rock mass did not extend to the Upper Devonian/Lower Mississippian gas field; and 2) there has been no detectable migration of gas or aqueous fluids to the Upper Devonian/Lower Mississippian gas field during the monitored period after hydraulic fracturing.

An electronic version of this report can be found at: http://www.netl.doe.gov/research/on-site-research/publications/featured-technicalreports and https://edx.netl.doe.gov/ucr.

Page 183

This report was difficult to find because the only article that mentioned the report did not give a link to it. If the report had proved that damage did occur due to hydraulic fracturing it probably would have been reported and repeated by all media outlets.

LW76...Oil About Ranching...Oil Prices
10-25-2014

The fields are white and ready to harvest. In the St. Lawrence area the situation can be described as black and white. Cotton on top and oil underneath. A tremendous amount of activity is taking place to harvest both crops. Both commodities seem to be in some confusion regarding the current, lower than anticipated, market price.

When you are up high, don't look down because it can be scary. It's easy to get dizzy. Last week an oilfield salesman said "If you know what the price of oil is today, don't tell me. I don't want to know." He wants to enjoy the good times just a little longer. When oil prices averaged just over $97 per barrel for about a year, it created something of a comfort zone as it appeared to have some stability. A ten percent rise above that was an indication of strength in the market. One individual received a nice raise just before the recent price break and told his wife about it. Her response was, "That's scary. We've been here before." She was not being superstitious, just speaking from experience of seeing one final surge before a fall. It's natural to want the good times to last just a little while longer.

Oil is really slick and it can be nerve wracking when it gets on that downhill slippery slope. Ignoring the oil price for several days does not seem to help and even covering one eye while looking doesn't provide much benefit. Oil has dropped more than 20% during the past several weeks. West Texas Intermediate Crude closed at $81.01 on October 24, 2014. The good news is that there seems to be some support at the $80 point with the price rebounding when it drops below that level. That's just a statement from trying to find some personal comfort in the situation and not a recommendation to buy it while it's cheap!

One of the often repeated questions is "At what price will drilling activity be affected?" The consensus, based on several recent articles and hearing guesstimates from people who have no insider or proprietary information appears that $70 is when the bean counters will really go into action. A similar question continues to be, "What is the break even price of oil?" That is often followed by a comment that they've heard that $70 is the break even price for oil. But it's like going from one cattle operation to another and learning about all of the variables. There are always some who are highly leveraged into a very high risk position while some are operating on a cash basis. There is not a one size fits all break even.

It is difficult to do an accurate comparison between the current oil boom and the one that some of us experienced a little over thirty years ago. I'm reminded of what my dad said many years ago about some of his old friends talking about the "good old days" and his opinion being that their comments were evidence of their poor memory. He went on to say that the one thing that was good about the so-called good old days was that they were younger then. The other oil boom was seen with my younger eyes of anticipation while this one is viewed with eyes dimmed with caution, based on experience.

Every boom, of whatever nature, seems to have a similar refrain about how it is different now because of being in a different economic era and that the old rules no longer apply. One of the big differences in the current oil boom is that interest rates are now much lower than the usurious rates experienced during the early eighties. It's been a while since the credit markets have really competed for capital and that may have had significant impact on the decision to place capital into productive, yet risky, enterprises.

At a glance, it appears that just maybe the boll weevil program and the fracking technology may have been just a little bit too successful at increasing the supply faster than the demand. Several years ago, somebody made a strong argument that perception is more important than reality. One frequent comment/question goes like this: "Since there is an oil glut, when are prices going to come down?" Everyone who has discussed this with me seems to be coming from the perception that our country is now producing a surplus of oil. They are unaware that we are still importing almost fifty percent of the oil that is being consumed in this country. We have a long way to go before our production can meet the current demand for oil.

Maybe it is perception more than reality when a little blip in the market has widespread impact. A few years ago, there was a wreck in the hog market that was blamed on more fat hogs being ready at one time than the processing plants could handle. It never was clear to me if that was just a regional event that caused a ripple effect. Was it a similar ripple effect from some recent sales of oil being heavily discounted because the pipelines were full? One report from several weeks ago was that some oil had been sold at about twenty dollars below the posted market because the producer(s) did not have transportation or storage capacity and had to do something with it. Very similar to a rancher hauling livestock to market based on the premise of "what will they give me for it". With the oil market now about the point where that discounted sale was made several weeks ago, the argument could be made (right or wrong) that the discounted sale caused by the clogged pipeline had the ripple effect leading to the current price. More questions than answers. Who would have thought that oil prices would drop while there is so much turmoil in the Mid-East?

LW77...OIL ABOUT RANCHING...ETHANOL 10-31-2014

West Texas Intermediate Crude Oil is slightly above $80 per barrel as October comes to a close. Questions outnumber answers as we look forward to cooler weather. If the price is based on supply and demand, why has the price fallen so much while we are still importing almost fifty percent of the oil that we consume? Are some of the Mid-East countries able to manipulate their production and distribution to cause short term price volatility? Watching oil and cattle prices has been a very interesting endeavor for the past couple of years.

While beef prices have remained high there are segments of the beef industry that have been hurting. A major packing plant closed and several feedlots have been reported to have either closed or cut back on numbers. With the cowherd numbers being down, the supply of feeder cattle has been reduced significantly. A strong case can be made for the fundamentals of supply and demand when it comes to the current beef prices.

The reduction in the feedlots and packers might be somewhat comparable to the rig count when considering that neither industry makes an instant response to market variation. At this time the rig count is holding about steady with the active rig count about ten percent higher than one year ago according to the Baker-Hughes report. At the end of October, there were 1,929 rigs at work in the U.S. The seven leading states for active drilling rigs are: Texas 901, Oklahoma 208, North Dakota 180, Lousiana 112, New Mexico 100, Wyoming 61 and California 46.

Each company probably has their own set of variables regarding their drilling programs. There may be some who have a knee jerk reaction to the immediate change in cash flow while others are set up for the long term. It's possible that some investors have been sitting on the sidelines waiting for what they believe is the right opportunity to get in. Drilling wells is somewhat like feeding cattle in that once you start, you are committed because there is not much of a market for half fed cattle or a half drilled well. This time lag contributes to the elasticity of supply and demand and the inevitable overreaction of the rebound effect. Those of us who are involved in the drilling operations will be listening for things like re-negotiating rig contracts and not re-newing contracts for underperforming and marginally rated rigs.

Most leases have an expiration date and require that drilling operations begin by a specific date in order to hold the lease. When prices drop, the competition for leases "on the fringe" seems to dissipate. One individual talks about how the $5,000 per acre lease offered on ten acres in the Barnett Shale was withdrawn when natural gas prices fell a few years ago.

One of the mysteries that continues to be puzzling involves ethanol. It seems that every article about ethanol is written BY someone who is heavily biased on one side or the other. Those with an oil company bias usually ignore the value of the byproducts from the distillation process. Those who are biased about corn seem to want to keep the focus on legislative and environmental issues. Neither side appears to be interested in using firm numbers to support a cost equivalent analysis that shows a true comparison. The definitive answer may be when we hear of farmers using ethanol to power tractors and other equipment. Has anybody heard any stories of workers in ethanol plants using some of the "surplus" product to power their vehicles like some of the gas plant hands were "accused" of using "drip gas" back in the day?

Some companies are claiming to be switching from diesel power to natural gas power for drilling rigs. (Is this comparable to corn farmers using ethanol for fuel?) Natural gas produced in the field might be more economical. Some good PR work can be done claiming to use cleaner fuel. Every load equivalent of natural gas piped to the rig is one less load of diesel delivered by truck. For those of us who travel the roads in the oil boom areas, we appreciate something positive to help with the traffic congestion.

A USDA report did provide some interesting numbers, even though it was not a complete comparative analysis. October 2014 corn prices were $3.37 per bushel compared to $4.46 one year ago. Ethanol price was $1.75 per gallon compared to $1.88 a year ago indicating that ethanol does not move in a one to one relationship with corn prices. Distiller Dried Grain at $98.80 per ton compared to $200 per ton one year ago showing another significant variable to enter into the equation. The report included that the yield amount for corn is 2.8 gallons of ethanol per bushel of corn. The corn also yields 17.75 pounds of Distillers Dried Grain per bushel.

Some of us still have concerns about a food grain being used for fuel. While visiting with a Missouri corn farmer on a flight out of Kansas City last summer, he brought up an interesting point about the benefit of having a market for moldy, and other inedible corn, through the ethanol plant.

If you know of any farmers using ethanol in their tractors or using natural gas from a methane generator from a hog or dairy barn, please let me know. Meanwhile, we'll keep on drilling. That is, as long as we are getting paid. It is not a hobby.

LW78...OIL ABOUT RANCHING...FRACKING VOTE

A vote to ban hydraulic fracturing passed in the City of Denton, Texas according to an Associated Press article press article in the Midland Reporter-Telegram. The article included the following statement: "For more than a decade, Denton has drawn its lifeblood from the huge gas reserves beneath its streets. The gas fields have produced $1 Billion in mineral wealth and more than $30 Million into city bank accounts." Is it just me, or does this sound something like biting the hand that feeds you?

There was statement indicating that existing permits being honored but there was no information regarding the current status or existence of any drilling and fracking projects. It was not specified on how this might affect leases that might be in place and not yet permitted. Many questions yet to be answered. What about the leases that have been paid but not yet permitted? Anyone with lease negotiations in progress might see the lease offers withdrawn abruptly. Will investors who have purchased mineral interests with hopes for future leases now have property that is basically worthless because it has been blocked by a vote?

Emotions seem to have outrun science on the fracking issue. A recent actual field study mentioned in this column showed no damage to have been caused by hydraulic fracking. Would it have made any difference if that study had been completed prior to calling for a vote on fracking?

Think about the impact that this could have on an entrepreneur who is in the business of leasing oil and gas prospects and pulling a group of investors together to develop and produce the property. The situation would be similar to someone who acquired a surface lease of some farmland within city limits and is voted out of business with a vote declaring that no farm equipment is allowed to operate within the city limits. Another vote comes along that prohibits livestock in the city limits so he can't plow it with a mule or even use the property for grazing.

This may open up a new can of worms due to infringement and economic impairment of private property. Not living in the vicinity of Denton may not be adequate to keep this from having some effect on the rest of us. It will be interesting to see if legal cases set some new precedence that impacts situations beyond the hydraulic fracking issue. Everyone who is concerned about private property issues may want to keep an eye on what is developing.

No information was provided whether those voting against fracking walked to the polls, rode bicycles or used genuine horsepower. Surely they would not have driven a petroleum powered vehicle to make such a vote. With winter coming soon, they just have a few days to get their solar heating equipment in place so that they will not be tempted to use any natural gas to heat their houses.

If it's any consolation to the anti-fracking crowd, I have no desire to do any drilling activity within any city. Some things, and some people, are better suited for the country.

Oil prices are something that are just not pleasant to talk about but can't be ignored. Being at the age that my long term plan and short term plan have converged, there is some desire to see this oil boom last just a little bit longer. Seeing oil below $78 the first week of November appears to have discredited the theory that we are in a new economic era where oil prices would remain above $100 for the next twenty years. Can't remember who made that statement a few months ago but do remember at the time thinking that he was in for a surprise. Some had claimed that the Saudis no longer had the capacity and market share to have a big impact on the market. With the increase in the U.S. production, it may now take a smaller percentage of increase from the Saudis to affect prices.

    There are some rumblings about some adjustments to drilling programs and re-working budgets. Many of those working in the drilling industry are hoping that this is the traditional fourth quarter slow-down and that it is temporary. With fifteen rigs in sight from where I am working, it looks like the boom is still on. Since friends, relatives and even strangers often blamed me for the high prices at the pumps, it will be my turn to take all the credit for increasing the supply and driving prices down and take the opportunity to suggest that they buy lunch to show their appreciation. Hopefully, cattle prices won't follow oil. It would be A shame to have to apologize for buying those first calf heifers.

LW79...OIL ABOUT RANCHING...MULES FOR ROYALTY

The old mule had another colt. That's my standard comment for a check that can be described as a dividend on the best horse and mule trade that was ever made in our family history. It's not a lot of money, just as mule colts are not worth a lot. It is some family history and is an example of something that can happen with oil and gas royalties.

In the early 1920's by Dad's stepfather made a trade for some horses and mules. As the story was told to me many years ago, it seems that he could not pass up the opportunity to buy some cheap horses and mules that had been traded in on tractors. He knew that tractors were only a passing fad and would not last because the tractors did not fertilize the fields as did work stock.

The transaction took place a few counties away and arrangements were made to put the horses and mules on pasture. It was not the first or last grazing deal that didn't work as planned. The tractor fad had not yet ended so the mule rally had not yet started. To say that he needed to divest of his investment in work stock was an understatement. Cash buyers for this particular class of horses and mules seemed to be non-existent.

While discussing his dilemma with some stranger he met on the trip to gather his stock, the stranger took his turn in the conversation to unload his own hard luck story. It seems that the stranger had somehow acquired a quarter section of land out in the dry desert country about a hundred miles or so west of San Angelo. Before the conversation was over, they had simply traded problems, sight unseen. The transaction was completed with the legal details of the transfer of the property recorded in the Glasscock County Courthouse. Unfortunately, the documents reveal only that "Ten Dollars and other valuable consideration" changed hands. There was some hope that there would be a note about how many horses and mules were involved, but that information was not recorded.

The oral history indicated that Dad's stepfather never saw the property. The timeline that can be verified is in the deed records in Glasscock County on a tombstone in the Crews cemetery recording his death in 1925, so we know the general timeframe. A side note about his death was something about using a prickly pear poultice to treat blood poisoning, which had resulted from a cut on one hand. Not all of those old home remedies were as effective as some would have us to believe. His death left a widow, my grandmother, with four children at home. Times were so hard back then that my dad never talked much about how rough it really was on the family. He did talk about the later years and said that the Depression of 1929 didn't have a major impact on them since they hadn't yet recovered from the 1919 Depression. No doubt that my grandmother desperately needed to sell the property in Glasscock County. During the late 20's, land buyers were almost as difficult to find as mule buyers had been a short time earlier. At the first opportunity, which was a few years later, my grandmother sold the property in Glasscock County. The records only show the customary "Ten Dollars and other valuable consideration", as was common in many land transactions so it is not known how much money she actually received for the property.

One day in 1953, my grandmother went to the mailbox and opened an envelope containing a check made out to her for $3,500, which was a lot of money at that time. (Also consider that 1953 was well into the Big Drought, to get an idea of how significant it may have been.) It turned out that the attorney who handled the sale of the property in Glassock County had reserved one half of the royalty interest in her name. She had no recollection of having been informed that half the royalty interest had been retained. Since it was royalty only, she was not involved in leasing the property. An oil well had been drilled and it took a few months to get the paperwork in order so it accumulated into a very nice check for her. No doubt she was surprised, very happy and graciously thankful.

Just a few days ago, which is also two generations later, with continual yet small production and with one-twenty-fourth of my Grandmother's interest, I opened an evelope with a check for $41. This is solid evidence that not all royalty owners are millionaires. It is also an example of how royalty interests can be divided and spread out. My memory is good enough that I can remember some times when I was several hundred dollars short of having $41, so I can still appreciate it. With Thanksgiving coming, it is a good reminder of so many things for which to be thankful.

After having worked as a drilling supervisor in eight states, I ended up working in Glasscock County. My curiosity was stirred about just where that property was located. While doing some research to pinpoint the location, it dawned on me that after all these years of the family receiving royalty income, nobody in our family had ever seen the property. Well, maybe I was the only one who ever thought about it. It was no big event but there was some satisfaction in locating the property and driving by it some ninety years after the trade. For some reason, it seemed necessary to see where all those "mule colts" had come from. Seems like there oughta be a good cowboy poem in there. Mules for Royalty. Where's Baxter or Red when we need them?

    Stay tuned. We'll take a look at what's happening to this oil boom.

LW80...Oil About Ranching...Oil Boom Update

The bloom is off the boom. West Texas Intermediate Crude Oil closed at $74.58 on November 19, 2014, down from the year's high point of $107.26 per barrel for about a thirty percent drop over a few months. The good news for some people is that the drop in fuel prices occurred at just the right time to provide some Christmas money in their budget. That was my incentive to go back to work in the oilfield "just a few days" to help finish a well. That was December of 2011 and I'm still trying to get some Christmas money put together.

According to the Baker-Hughes rig count there were 568 rigs working in the Permian Basin this week compared to 470 one year ago. Total for Texas was 902 now and 825 a year ago. The total U.S. count is 1,928 rigs up from 1,762 in one year. It seems like a spoke breaks about the same time that everybody gets on the bandwagon.

It was interesting to see that Canada has 402 rigs running now compared to 401 a year ago. No mention of why the count has remained flat for our neighbors to the north. One reason may be that several Canadian rigs are now operating in the U.S. You have probably noticed that the Keystone pipeline project is in the news and the halls of Congress. Could it be that the lack of pipeline for export may have curbed the drilling activity in Canada?

When listening to the news that seems to either be pro-oil or anti-oil in their opinions about the pipeline, there are some things to consider. The oil industry is not one dimensional. The components of exploration, production, refining, transportation and marketing do not necessarily always work together in harmony with the other's best interest any more than the cattle industry components of cow-calf, stockers, feeders, truckers, packers and grocery stores. Sometimes it seems that those who would be assumed to be in harmony have the most friction. When working for big oil, it became evident sometimes that the competition from outside companies was not nearly to be feared as much as internal battles between departments.

All of that just to say that the Keystone pipeline may not benefit the U.S. drilling industry. The fundamental purpose for the pipeline is to increase supply which theoretically will reduce prices. The designed beneficiary of a pipeline that provides additional product is the consumer and not the driller. It seems that some people are reacting to the idea of an oil pipeline as if this is the first time that they have ever heard of such a thing. Maybe it is.

A few months ago the prognosticators seemed to all be singing from the same sheet of music. Oil prices would remain high. Hundred dollar a barrel oil was the "new normal" because we were into a new economic era and the old rules no longer applied. Just look at all the rigs and people that are working and all the new rigs that are on order with nobody knowing who will operate them when delivered. This oil boom was different and no end in sight. Without writing it on the calendar, there's no way to verify that the slide in oil prices started the same day that some predictor was going on about how the boom had leveled out and would last for at least twenty years. Maybe they were a few days apart, but it was close.

It was not comforting to read on Saturday that some

CEO's were saying on Tuesday that they had projects where they would stay active in drilling and development even if oil is $80. They weren't quoted as to their intentions if oil dropped below $76 by Friday. One of my favorites was a professor at some university (where else?) who said that it would be the second quarter of next year before the drop in oil prices affected drilling budgets. Maybe he will have the opportunity to explain this to some rig hands who posted job searches on a website this week when their rig went down.

The (im)perfect storm may have come together. The boom plateaued on strong demand with many fundamentals supporting high oil prices and the enthusiasm was contagious. Maybe the boom just lost its momentum about the time that Saudi Arabia decided that they did not want to lose market share. It sounds like the prognosticators turned a page and are singing harmony about how it will take two years for oil prices to recover, unless some world event causes a market change. (How can I get one of those dream jobs at a university that pays a person to make such predictions?)

As with any boom type activity, costs have gone up and seem to have been out of control. It may be that it is simply time for the "fall works" and that some culling will take place. Some contracts will probably be re-negotiated and some rates adjusted. My favorite quote of the week was seen in the Midland-Reporter Telegram in an article about the Executive Oil Conference: "Currently the industry has seen oil prices fall 25% while costs have risen 30%. The industry has not done a good job of capital discipline." Credited to Travis Stice of Diamondback Energy. A rather striking statement. Sort of had a bite to it.

LW84...OIL ABOUT RANCHING...CHRISTMAS

Christmas day on a drilling rig is about 96 hours long. One way to encourage workers who are stuck out on a rig at this time is to remind them that it's much better to be working on Christmas Day than to be at home without a job. Having a job at Christmas is much better than looking for one. In June, who would have thought that oil would drop $40 by Christmas and that the oil boom would switch to panic mode? Some people in the drilling industry who are on the front end of the slow down will be spending Christmas at home wondering when and where the next job will be. Some may be like the man from another state who came to participate in the oil boom and said that he was making four times as much money but expenses were four times as much so he couldn't tell that he had gained anything. My guess is that he won't be back for the next go round, whenever that may be. Hopefully, those who have been so busy working didn't have time to spend all the money that they earned and now enjoy some time off and focus on what is really important.

It was one of those 96 hour long Christmas Days out on a rig several years ago that got me to thinking about the shepherds who were chosen to deliver a message so many centuries ago. Having grown up raising sheep, even though I never had seen a real shepherd, there should have been some understanding about the professional and social status of shepherds. Their position did not place them among the religious elite and scholars of their time. In today's terms, their resume probably would not have shown qualifications to be selected to deliver such an important message.

What if the timing and location of history had been changed and the big event happened this century rather than twenty centuries ago? With no shepherds "abiding in their field at night" who might be selected? Consider what it would be like for a group of roughnecks on morning tour to have been the individuals who were chosen to be visited by an angel. Surely, the intellectual elite would be offended by not having been selected and would give no credibility to the night crew coming off the rig looking for the motel at the edge of town with horse stables out back.

Having heard the account of the shepherds all of my life, it never crossed my mind that they might not have wanted to go to town and tell about the angel coming to see them. Changing the scenario to a crew of roughnecks brings up the question about how readily that they would accept the news. Would they have been all enthusiastic and immediately left for town or would they stop and talk this over among themselves? Did the thought cross their mind that probably nobody would believe their story? One of the shepherds may have had a recent experience where people didn't believe that he killed a wolf at fifty paces with his slingshot. Much like a roughneck might be ridiculed about his claim killing a deer at three hundred yards with an open sight 30/30. If they didn't believe that, who would believe this? Sometimes even when it is true and happened to you, there is some hesitation about telling about something that might be met with disbelief.

Were they so compelled that they simply had to go without question? Would it have made any difference regarding the birth that orchestrated history if the shepherds had decided to stay with the sheep? It's easy to imagine that the roughnecks working night shift might want to sort of ignore the situation and let the daylight crew handle it in case the angel came back. Roughnecks working the night shift did not invent passing the buck but have developed it into a fine art. Maybe the shepherds just went as they were instructed.

History did not record the names of the shepherds. Maybe it was because the message was so much more important than the messengers. By having the non-descript shepherds make the journey and tell their story, it was all about the message and not the messengers. For some reason, they were selected to be part of the greatest story ever told.

The story of Hanukkah also comes to mind about the time that there was only enough oil for one day but the lamp burned for eight days. We can be thankful that we didn't run out of oil because the country that runs on oil can't afford to run short. Of the many things for which to give thanks is the ingenuity and tenacity of American workers who increased production so much in the past three years that it shook the world markets.

Maybe the drop in oil prices will allow us to catch our breath and take another look at what is really important. As we get ready to close the books on the final scene of the great oil boom of 2014, let's make this Christmas a celebration of Faith, Family and Friends.

LW86...Oil About Ranching...Chronology of the Oil Bust

First the good news. For those who have been wishing for lower gasoline prices, your dreams have come true. Then not quite as good; for those who run diesel powered vehicles, you are paying about a dollar more per gallon for diesel than for gasoline. That price disparity is a reminder that our elected officials and the bureaucrats who they appoint have not been doing us any favors regarding diesel fuel. Do some research before blaming the oil companies on that one.

Way back in the summer of 2014, West Texas Intermediate Crude Oil was selling for $107 per barrel. Now in January 2015, it seems like that was a long time ago. Times were good and there was no end in sight. Many of us working in the drilling industry were making more money than we ever dreamed and were caught up in the euphoria of the oil boom. Although I stayed constant with the same prediction made in 1981 "that the boom will end and it will happen sooner and be worse than we can imagine right now". However, I was beginning to feel that maybe this was somewhat different and that this boom would last much longer.

The fatigue was setting in and I needed a break from the stressful job as a drilling consultant. But my plan was to work until May of 2015 when my wife plans to retire from teaching. In March I ordered my "retirement boots" from one of the custom boot shops. With a fourteen month waiting list, the boots would be ready about the same time that I planned to step away from the drilling rigs and do some traveling. At least we had a definite target and had set some goals. A short trip to Cloudcroft late in the summer for some cool days and a few relaxing nights and good meals at the old Lodge helped us get rejuvenated to face the next several months.

Physically, I needed a break but was unwilling to consider taking time off from a job that was paying so much. My wife was not sure that she could handle the stress of another year of teaching but needed that one more year to meet retirement qualifications. As we looked back at how fast the previous twenty years had flown by, we were convinced that we could hang on for almost another year. And so began the chronology of an oil bust.

Along about September, a pay raise was delivered that was beyond my imagination. Greed can induce adrenalin. Not only was I convinced that I can't quit now, I began to question the plan to take off in May of 2015. The old lesson to not quit milking 'til the cow goes dry was coming back to me. My wife's comment about the raise was cautious, wondering if that "might not be a good sign; seems like we've been through this scenario before."

Oil prices began to slide a little in October. Many of us talked too much about oil prices and watched the downturn begin. Consensus was that it was only a temporary correction or a normal fourth quarter adjustment of no big concern. In many conversations about the status of the oil field, my comment was that I hoped that both the boom and I would last at least until those new boots are completed. Several times I was told that there was no way the boom would end before my new boots were completed.

In November, here came the frightening words

"Nobody here has anything to worry about." Having heard those at least once per decade beginning in the 70's, I knew that it was a true statement even though my interpretation of truth was not exactly what the speaker intended. There are times when the speaker is trying more to convince himself than the audience. Based on the admonition that worrying doesn't help, it's true that there was no need to worry.

December rolled around and some rigs were being laid down and projects were being cancelled. One night about 2AM, I climbed down from a cement truck after monitoring the displacement and noticed how I was having to pay close attention to every step and handhold on that ladder and had the thought that maybe I shouldn't be doing this anymore. Many consultants and drilling supervisors deceive themselves into believing that they are somebody special due to their pay level and rank in the pecking order. In reality, consultants are at best nothing more than day workers with a somewhat rare skill and at worst are nothing more than some rusty old rental equipment that will be sent back to wherever it came from whenever no longer needed. It was not unexpected when that call came to me in mid-December that the round up was over.

It had been a good run. Many readers will remember that my part in this boom started in December of 2011 when I went out "just to work a few days to help finish a well." It was now time to go home and I was ready. It was nice to not have to worry through Christmas about how much longer the boom would last for me.

Sometimes it works out so that we are exactly where we need to be at the very time that we are needed. Following a Christmas trip to the in-laws in Missouri, my wife began to feel uncomfortable, then gradually worse the following day and then began to have a fever. After agreeing that maybe she should go to the Emergency Room on December 28, we made a quick trip to Abilene. After all night in the emergency room followed by an MRI, it was discovered that she had a ruptured appendix and needed surgery immediately. She came through the surgery okay and spent a week in the hospital. Now at home, she is making progress every day, even though it will be a long recovery. She was told that she would have to stay home and miss school for six weeks. She needed a break from school but this was difficult way to get it. Miraculously, it has renewed her spirit and she says that she is no longer worried about school. If the doctor cut out that worry, he's quite a surgeon and I'm going to recommend him for medal.

For several days I was unconcerned about the price of oil and the rig count. This old rusty piece of rental equipment had more important things to do than dig another hole in the ground. We have so much for which to be thankful. Stay tuned and we'll try to catch up on what's happening in the oil patch next week.

LW87...OIL ABOUT RANCHING...ANALYSTS? POUND A YEAR GAIN

In reading many articles by various analysts, it is usually more of a concern about what is being left out than what is being put into their article. Based on some of their analysis, they could make the case that since I've averaged a pound of gain per year since graduation that in another forty plus years at the current rate of gain that my weight will be adequate for being a competitive steer wrestler. It may be an absurd comparison, but so is the idea that any boom will never end.

In June, business was good and the optimism was contagious. Leases were hitting all time highs, irrigation water for cotton was being diverted to drilling and fracking, a bunch of high school drop outs were making over a hundred grand a year, businesses were expanding and just like the highway construction in downtown Garden City, there was no end in sight.

Watching the oil boom from my front row seat as a drilling consultant was a combination of excitement and a small hint of warning. Sometimes I tried to get a grasp of how things had gone from me being told that I was "too young and inexperienced" to the point where I was almost too old but my experience was of such value that the pay rate was beyond what I could have ever imagined. The fatigue was catching up with me. I needed to take a break but knew even if this oil boom lasted another twenty years as some predicted, that I couldn't participate much longer and better get all I could while the getting was good.

LW88...OIL ABOUT RANCHING...LEASE IMPACT.
CLINE. 1/26/2015

It was a sure thing that one would not have to look very far to find someone who had a lease negotiation cancelled. Didn't even have to look, just saw an old friend at a cattle auction and he told about a lease that fell through. There was something about some minor wording that he wanted changed and a little trip that he took. He said that those few days of delay were right when oil prices dropped significantly. After several attempts to contact the leasing entity, he was informed that the offer to lease his property had been withdrawn. The verbal agreement for an amount about the value of a really nice new pick-up turned out to be worthless.

Also received word from a lifetime acquaintance down on the coast who had been involved in the process of selling some inherited royalty interest. Again, a verbal agreement had been made regarding a written offer. The purchasing entity was doing research on the ownership and had hit a snag at the courthouse in searching through documents. She had the basic history of the property but there was a missing link in an estate record, or something of the sort. Now in her eighties, the lady was wanting to sort out some things to simplify her estate. The offer to purchase was simply dropped. That deal was almost four times as much as the lease mentioned above. Probably not a lifestyle changing event in either case but each party could probably have put the money to good use.

Some of the stories that are being told about leases expiring are reminders of what happened in the eighties. One particular property of which I am aware did not have another offer for more than twenty years. An acquaintance with some property in the Barnett Shale has not had another offer since a lease offer was withdrawn several years ago. Some of the prospects probably don't look as good as they did a year ago. However, just like the cattle feeders who keep on feeding through the down times, there are probably some people working oil leases to put themselves in good position for when things turn around.

It was reported by AP and Bloomberg that a Japanese corporation had written down its investment in Cline Shale leases to the tune of just over $1.5 Billion. That sounds like it could be a project to study wealth redistribution via the risks associated with free market capitalism. The article didn't mention how much of that investment was in the form of direct leases, drilling expenses or other technical and professional services. Indications are that most of the Cline Shale is in or adjacent to the Permian Basin. There was a serious amount of cash that went into several counties between Abilene and Pecos. A chamber of commerce economist might could put a "multiplier effect" on that to estimate how much of an overall impact that it may have had on the area. With all of the drilling that has occurred, no doubt some analysts are looking at the production rates and are sorting out the winners and losers.

The Baker-Hughes rig report showed that the U.S. rig count for the week ending January 23 was 1,633 which was down 43 from the previous week and down 144 from one year ago. A friend in Midland sent a picture of a drilling company yard where they are stacking rigs in the yard with the derricks up, rather than laid over, so that they will be able to put more rigs into the yard. It sounded like mostly a negative statement but one advantage of having the derricks up is that the components could be functioned periodically to keep the equipment maintained and ready to go when needed. It is a big, reputable company with a good history (yes, I'm biased - based on experience) and no doubt they are planning ahead.

One of the things to keep in mind, with the rig count falling, is that there are still a lot of rigs working and they are drilling more wells in less time than they were just a few years ago. Better bits and vast amounts of new technology have been very beneficial. No doubt that all kinds of cost cutting efforts are being implemented. One service company owner told me that he was told that he would have to cut costs by a large percentage to keep working for a certain operator. He said that percentage exceeded his gross margin and he could not send crews and equipment out knowing that he was going to lose money on the deal.

Several years ago, I was in a situation where "the bean counters showed up" and everything was being scrutinized. The drilling manager said that we needed to come up with some ways to reduce costs. It was a nearly impossible situation because everything had been controlled "by the office" and the contractural terms and conditions were completely out of the hands of the field personnel. More than 95% of the costs were locked in. We field supervisors were in a situation where they wanted us to make some big cuts. Sort of like skinning a bear with one of those plastic picnic knives. Sometimes it's pretty obvious that something has just about run its course.

One of the saddest things about the current downturn is the effect on people who are suddenly out of a job. Not only does it affect them and their families, it also represents some technical training that may be lost to the industry. They may have been at the point in the learning curve that they were developing some expertise and really becoming valuable to their employer. In some cases, that training will be lost when a worker relocates and gets into another job. When activity picks up, some new people will have to be trained to fill some of the jobs.

One of the good things that has occurred with all of the drilling is that there is a significant amount of production. Even though oil prices are down, there is still a lot of work to be done by people in the production department who get the oil to market. The drilling people are something like the old time trail drivers who were flamboyant and got all the attention while production people do all of the routine activity that keeps the system working. It's just another chapter in human history about some being explorers and some being settlers.

LW89...Oil About Ranching...Oil Consumption
1-31-2015

 West Texas Intermediate Crude closed just over $46 per barrel and the U.S. Rig Count for the week ending 1-31-2015 was at 1,543 which is down by 90. Is this the reward for improved technology and performance? Looks like a lot of people did such a good job that they worked themselves out of a job. Supply and demand can be very confusing. There's more than one way to look at it.

 It was a pleasure to cross trails with a young man who represents the third generation that I have known in a nice family. He quickly began telling me that he had a horse that I needed, which caught me by surprise because I was absolutely unaware of any such need. He went on to describe the horse as being only 14.2 hands tall, fourteen years old and very gentle. As he continued on, it dawned on me that he was describing a horse that was "old man gentle". While explaining to him that I was totally unaware of having any need for another horse, I agreed to take a look at the horse just in case somebody showed up needing such an animal. (For the uninitiated this "just gonna look" is a typical reaction for the unfortunate carriers of the equine reactive disorder which often affects decision making.) The horse looked very nice, and knowing the owner, there was no concern on my part that the horse might have been misrepresented in any way.

 The next day while looking at the last colt we had raised, I thought about the admonition of an old friend who suggested that I should re-examine my birth certificate by paying particular attention to the date and consider making some adjustments in some of the things I continue to attempt. Maybe I did need to try out that 14 year old horse instead of dreaming about what the yearling might do in a couple of years. Just one phone call and the next day the horse was delivered to my place for me to try out. After behaving and performing exactly as described, my "need" for the horse was verified. Plus, he is my favorite color. Gentle.

Oil prices falling so rapidly seems to defy logic pertaining to supply and demand. There is something about the height of horses which may relate to the economic term "elasticity of supply and demand" as in how it pertains to the fact that a specific percentage change in supply may not have the same percentage change in demand, or price. A horse that is 15.1 is only 5% taller than one that is 14.2. Yet it now seems to take 90% more effort to mount such a tall beast. Definitely not a one to one ratio of height to effort required. A small percentage increase in the amount of horse results in a huge percentage increase in the effort required to mount (compounded by age). Not sure about the mathematical formula, but the knees don't lie!

The recent sixty percent drop in oil prices did, without warning, fulfill the prediction that someday the oil prices would break and that it would happen sooner and be worse than we could imagine. History, rather than current events or market analysis, was the basis for the prediction. So much for the roar of the crowd claiming that this time it was different and a new economic era was in place. For some reason, the term "new economic era" now seems to sound more like "new economic error".

The U.S. oil consumption in 2013 averaged about

18.9 million barrels of oil per day. (Don't trust my numbers. Please do your own research. As always, all applicable disclaimers apply.) The U.S. oil production rate was reported by Bloomberg to be 11 million barrels per day for the first quarter of 2014. We are only producing 58% of the oil that we consume. This country is still importing 42% of the oil that we use. For some interesting conversation, just ask somebody, anybody, about the U.S. oil production and consumption to see if they are aware that the U.S. is still having to import oil. I continue to be mystified by the number of people who believe that the U.S. is literally in an oil glut of excess production. If you really want to get someone started, do like some of the big media people and start off with a presumptuous and misleading question such as, "with the current excess production of oil in the U.S., should companies be allowed to export oil?"

With all due respect and a personal preference towards self preservation, the name and position of the public official will not be revealed. There are, however, certain elected officials in Texas that we would expect to have a firm grasp of the numbers regarding oil production and consumption. It might be said that in one case it is part of the job description. I sincerely hope that the official was quoted out of context and/or that the writer mis-understood exactly what was being said. The comment about going from a shortage to a surplus sure sounded like he believed that we, that is the U.S., now had a surplus of oil. Now there are certain places like the Eagle Ford, North Dakota and Barnhart that do have a surplus in their immediate area. That does not mean that the nation has a surplus. However, it may add to the perception of the general public that a nation wide oil surplus does exist. My perception many years ago was that when the rails were taken up between Abilene and Ballinger, that the railroads were going out of business. Didn't happen. Perceptions can be misleading.

Speaking of perception. Drilling consultants are often perceived to have the top job in the oil field but in reality most of us are independent contractors with no benefits and in reality know that we are nothing more than rusty old rental equipment under the "expendable" category. Maybe that is how some trail drivers and stagecoach drivers felt when their industry slowed.

LW90...Oil About Ranching...Holding Oil Until Price Goes Up?

One reader asked an interesting question regarding why oil producers would sell oil at current low prices instead of holding it and waiting for prices to rise. He stated that he didn't understand the oil business and that it might not be an accurate comparison as to whether an operator could hold the oil for later sale similar to the way that he as a rancher might hold some cattle for sale at some later date, when the price goes up.

One of the biggest differences in a rancher selling livestock is that a rancher can sell everything that he raises on one day. Calves can be sold at early weaning or carried over with steers being sold as long yearlings and the heifers kept until they are bred. From a marketing opportunity there is a large window for selling calves at anytime from five months or twenty-four months of age. Ten different ranchers will probably have at least a dozen reasons for marketing the way that they do and most of those reasons are related to grass and money.

Oil is produced daily and sold every day, so there is a continually moving process. It's probably more accurate to compare oil production and sales to a dairy operation than a ranch. Some small producers may have some excess storage capacity to hold several days production, but by design or by default, every day is sale day for an oil producer. About the only way for an oil producer to hold the oil and wait for a higher price is to shut in the wells. In the past, there have been reports of some producers doing just that. This is based on the assumption that the oil is in the ground and will stay in the ground and not go anywhere. Another option is to set the timers so that pumping units run less time and produce less oil. If a well is flowing it can be choked down to reduce the flow. Many of us hold to the opinion of never shutting in a flowing well based on our experience that the well never comes back as good as it was. This is another one of those situations where engineering theory and experience may differ.

If a rancher holds calves over they continue to grow and he continues to produce his product for that one day that he eventually sells. However, if a forty barrel per day well is held back to twenty barrels that does not mean that the stored production can be retrieved at will. That is, due to the lack of porosity and permeability of the formation, it cannot be cranked up to produce eighty or one hundred barrels per day to make up for the restricted, or delayed production.

The operating expenses and overhead for an oil company occur every day and the cash flow of income and expenses is a vicious cycle. A short term interruption can cause many problems. Even the extreme measure of shutting in wells and laying off employees will not stop all expenses. A company may lay off a large percentage of employees but still keeps enough to keep the production systems operating and the office operating. Maintaining the system so that production can be increased when the price rises may require that the operation continues for several months at a loss.

An oil operator may have the same dilemma about partially shutting in production that a rancher may encounter if he believes there is more opportunity to hold the calves over for several months. The existence of a note at the bank may have the greatest impact on the decision.

Just from observation and no privileged information, it does appear that some oil companies were drilling more wells instead of piling up cash in the bank while oil prices were high. It kept reminding me of 1974 when some cattle feeders had re-invested all of their profits into equity for more cattle to feed. After starting off with one pen of cattle they had built up to three pens. They had three times as much equity but also three times as much debt. With hundred dollar a barrel crude oil being the new accepted standard only a few months ago (but it seems like a LONG time ago now) the incentive was to drill, drill, drill. With only few rare exceptions, the daily expenses of drilling a well far exceed the daily income that the well will provide. Just for an example, if a well is really good and will pay out in six months it seems like it is highly profitable. However, if the rig is drilling one well per month the production income is not keeping up with the expenses. Of course, it is all dependent upon the overall production of an oilfield and how much capital is on hand, but the point is that almost any drilling program can grow to the point that it is non-sustainable just like the cattle feeder rolling profits into equity and increasing his position.

In both situations it was a calculated risk based on the market staying above a certain point. When oil prices dropped to half the cash flow changed that hypothetical payout from 12 months to 24 months. Suddenly, the long term drilling project is shut down due to short term cash needs to pay the expenses and bank notes.

Then there is the human factor of decision making. The decision makers may be investing their own money or it may be that they are managing it for stockholders. Stock options may be a major portion of a manager's compensation, so there is incentive to keep things looking as good as possible for as long as possible. Then there are some who hedged (contracted) their production. Similar to the rancher they sold several months production in one day. By doing so they may miss some upside opportunity but at least they survive and keep on drilling.

My partial explanation probably just adds to the confusion. With predictions that oil prices will be somewhere between twelve and two hundred dollars and the admonition to act accordingly, it is a confusing situation. Meanwhile, the week ending Feb 6, 2015 saw another 87 rigs go down in the U.S. resulting in a total of 1,456 rigs now working. That number is down 548 from one year ago. West Texas Intermediate crude crept up a little over $50.

LW91...OIL ABOUT RANCHING...HENDRICKS

There are many ways that petroleum has impacted our lives and it has been taken for granted by most of my generation, who were born in the middle of the previous century. Many of us can look back to our grandparents who lived for many years with only horse and mule power for transportation and without indoor plumbing and electricity. Coal is what put the industrial age on track but it was petroleum that put it on the road and in the air. Most of our necessities and luxuries are produced and/or delivered by petroleum. Sometimes, it is good to stop and think about how these things have been provided.

Welcoming in the New Year and spending several days in and around Hendrick Medical Center in Abilene, while my wife was recovering from appendicitis surgery, provided an opportunity to really appreciate many of the benefits of the industrial revolution and technology that has been developed. Although surgery for a ruptured appendix may now be considered routine, there can be complications and there were several scary hours during the recovery process. Remembering the stories that my parents told of them each having appendectomies several years before I was born was not something that I liked to think about. Back then, the mortality rate was high for that type of surgery.

Going back a little further, my maternal great grandfather was a medical doctor in the late 1800's and early 1900's. Just to think that he carried most of the known medical technology in a small case in his buggy. It was a reminder of the advances that have been made in a relative short period of history. My work around the massive equipment used in the drilling industry gives me a great deal of appreciation for the research and development that has been required to develop current medical technology.

On a drilling rig, there are many concerns about various pieces of equipment where failure can result in catastrophic injuries. There is a reason that we pay particular attention to the drilling line. Drilling line is the cable that runs on the hoisting mechanism that raises and lowers the drill pipe and bit. The drilling line use is documented in hours and replaced on schedule with a higher priority than changing oil in the engines. Thinking about quality control and inspection processes that we use on a rig was not really a comforting thing when looking at the tiny tubes and wires that were serving various functions for my wife as she lay in the hospital bed. The only thing more amazing than the medical technology was the people who were involved in all of the processes. To say that we are thankful for them is an understatement.

Since Hendrick Hospital had been around a long time before I was born, it was natural to take it for granted and not think much about the history of how it started. There was some memory of hearing that there was some oil money involved. There are numerous sources that provide some history of how the hospital began in the early 1900's and like many institutions it was in extreme financial need in the mid-thirties during the depth of the depression. Similarly, Mr. and Mrs. T.G. Hendrick were facing tough times in the ranching business in Winkler County and some reports claim they were about to lose the ranch.

Then oil was discovered on the ranch and that

saved the ranch. Not only did it save the ranch but provided them with the funds to help rescue the hospital in Abilene that was in extreme financial need. There are numerous accounts telling about the hospital being renamed "Hendrick" in appreciation of their supporting gift. They also started the children's home that is also named after them. I would like to read some more detailed history about them. Their legacy is a lesson in giving. Apparently it was another case of not only what was done but that it was also at just the right time. The modern facility has not departed from its roots. Their mission statement says it all. Not politically correct.

One of the comments about the Hendrick oil discovery was about it being the first field to be drilled with rotary rigs rather than cable tool rigs. It got me to comparing that advance in technology to the advances that we've seen recently with the horizontal drilling and fracking. Could it be that those newly developed rotary drilling rigs made the difference in those wells being drilled just in time to provide the funds that were needed? For the time it was possibly as much of an industry change as fracking is now.

Anyone who cusses the oil industry should be reminded not to do it while receiving treatment at Hendricks, or any number of other medical facilities whose history is written in oil Sort of like telling people to not cuss farmers and ranchers with their mouth full of food.

For the week ending Feb 25, 2015, the Midland Reporter Telegram reports WT Intermediate crude at $52.78. Ninety eight rigs were stacked out in the U.S. last week leaving the total U.S. rig count at 1,358 and 1,298 of those are on land. This is the first time in five years that the U.S. land rig count has been below 1,300.

Diesel is still sixty cents to a dollar a gallon higher than gasoline and I counted thirty-two dead skunks on the road between Barnhart and Mertzon. Those two statistics share a common denominator.

LW92...OIL ABOUT RANCHING...ABSURDITIES
2—22—2015

More oil is being produced now than was being produced a year ago even though fewer oil drilling rigs are at work. Milk production is up even though there are fewer steers on feed in the major cattle feeding regions.

The two previous statements have something in common. Both infer some idea of production analysis with related cause and effect. Those of us who are involved in the production of anything are concerned about the perceptions that may impact customer's decisions. How many beef producers watch a news report about a possible "e coli outbreak" and yell at the television, "COOK IT!" ? Of course, we all want to prevent any such problem, but in the event it happens (even if caused by the consumer's improper handling) we want the news person to remind everyone that properly cooking to an adequate temperature will probably eliminate the danger.

The leading statement about oil production being up, even though rig count in that area was down from a year earlier came from an article that may have been written with the intent to provide some analysis of the current situation. The second statement of absurdity popped into my mind as an example of how a perception may be created through the use of unrelated cause and effect. As tempting as it is to elaborate, it's best to pass on explaining the statement about milk production and steers on feed.

The statement about oil production being up, even

with fewer drilling rigs at work may create the wrong perception. The impression could be left that drilling rigs produce oil. Another possibility is that efficiency and technology has been improved so that more oil can be produced with fewer rigs. It is true that rigs are more efficient at drilling wells and that with more wells being drilled, then more oil can be produced. It's a reminder that the majority of the population is not aware that drilling rigs are generally not producing oil* but are creating the wellbore through which oil will be produced after the drilling rig is moved away. So, the higher rig count last year means that there are now more wells to produce oil. With few exceptions, drilling rigs consume more oil than is produced during the drilling operation. The consumption of fifty barrels of diesel fuel per day while drilling is common.

The rig count going down does not have an immediate impact on oil production. It is a delayed reaction. Even though the rig count is going down, the wells that have been drilled recently are being completed and connected to the production facilities. The good news is that there is still a substantial amount of work to be done after the drilling rigs are gone. Wells normally do not last forever and new wells must be drilled to maintain and increase production. In the past few years, much of the drilling industry has performed so efficiently that it has been to their own detriment. There is nothing like working yourself out of a job.

Another problem about incorrect perceptions about the petroleum industry was very obvious in a recent television program with high suspense and drama. One of the issues involved in the drama was a leaking pipeline with the perception that the company "did not care" about the leaking pipeline. The thought police can run wild with the accusation "they don't care". It was distracting to realize that the general public watching that TV show could be indoctrinated with the idea that a company wouldn't care if a pipeline leaked. It becomes an emotional argument of "care vs. don't care". The viewer was left with the presumption that a company would not "care" about a leaking pipeline unless they get caught. Let's leave the emotion alone and look at the goal and objective for a pipeline. The goal of the pipeline is to move a product from one place to another with the objective to make a profit.

With all of the "they don't care" accusations made toward companies, one thing that they "do care" about is profit. A leaking pipeline loses money. The company has a vested interest in having a secure pipeline with no leaks. It is in the best interest of pipeline companies to use the latest technology to monitor lines for leaks and have the capability to isolate a section where a leak occurs in order to limit the amount spilled. Was it intentional indoctrination that the program included the leaky pipeline scenario while some politicians are doing more damage than a leaky pipeline while delaying a project that would provide jobs and tax revenue?

Forty-eight more rigs were idled in the U.S. for the week ending February 20, 2015 according to the Baker-Hughes report. That leaves 461 fewer rigs at work than one year ago at this time. West Texas Intermediate Crude is still a little over fifty dollars per barrel.

*In some formations a wellbore may produce oil during the drilling operation. Financially this can be very beneficial due to quick return on investment. For the workers, the risk increases substantially due to the exposure of flammable oil and gas being produced.

LW94...Oil About Ranching...Rig to Scrap Yard

It is always good to hear from readers of this column and a recent email from a young engineer was no exception. Graduating from college and going to work for a growing oil company during the upswing of the oil boom was exciting and promising. Growing up on a farm probably did more to prepare him for the drop in oil prices than anything that he was taught at the university.

He mentioned a drilling rig that had been working for his company and that was an old rig that had not been adequately maintained and that it would be taken out of service and go to the scrap yard when finished with drilling the current well. Maybe that particular rig is going to be scrapped but the statement stirred some memories of similar rigs that needed to have been scrapped. When times get tough and most operators are demanding to cut costs, the old rigs are where cost cutting can be more easily justified. The combination of lower investment and available spare parts from other old rigs may make the older rig more competitive when cost cutting is the priority.

Letting an almost new drilling rig sit in the yard while an old rig is being sent out to work may seem like a poor choice but a drilling company may be more willing to reduce rates on an old rig than on a newer one. This can also be one of the things that slows the development of technology. The newer rigs have more high tech and higher investment equipment that also typically is higher maintenance. One of the worst things about seeing some of the newer hi-tech rigs being put in storage yards is realizing the impact that it will have on Research and Development. When cost cutting takes place, the R&D budget is often among the first to be hit.

It is common to think about manufactured items being tested, tried and proven. One of the differences with drilling rigs is that there are few which are identical. While trucks are built by the thousands, rig orders are often in the single digits. Even the most common components that may be used on various rigs are probably numbered at only a few hundred. A modest improvement in any component may not be compatible with other similar items that are in service.

The most rapid developments have occurred in the computerized equipment and operating systems. Sometimes when high tech meets hardware it's not pretty. Tiny circuits that are common with computerization are not always compatible with extreme conditions including vibration and temperature changes. One example involved a problem with a top drive unit which includes all of the computer and hydraulic connections. The decision was made to change out a major component instead of continuing to try and make repairs in the field. It was "exactly the same" and was shipped in from several hundred miles away.

After all of the components were changed out, it was discovered that the protective back cover would not fit. The replacement that was thought to be "exactly the same" was a "new and improved" version that had slightly larger connections to better withstand the extreme operating environment. It was one of those times where a half inch difference was like a half mile because it wasn't something that could be easily modified by a welder. This took almost two extra days to complete the repairs and replacement. The fact that it happened during the drilling process meant that all of the daily expenses continued on.

A current photo of a rig yard with about twenty of the newer high tech rigs that had been taken out of service raises the question about where are the people who worked on the rigs? The computer technicians with the skills and advanced training who can work on the newer type rigs are very few. They are also among a rare few who have been willing to work long hours day and night while spending much time away from home. Anyone who has paid attention to the law of the jungle will realize that these workers are survivors and will not be the first to starve. They will find other work and may not be available when the drilling activity increases.

West Texas Intermediate Crude was $49.61 per barrel on March 6, 2015. The U.S. rig count according to Baker-Hughes was down by 75 to 1,192 which is 600 fewer rigs working than one year ago.

LW95...OIL ABOUT RANCHING...OIL INVENTORIES INCREASING

Ranchers and farmers probably understand, and practice, the concept of increasing inventory volumes when prices are low. Whether buying supplies for future use or holding current products in hopes for a better price in the future, the accumulation of inventory when prices are low seems to be a common occurrence. Recently there have been some articles about the amount of crude oil in storage increasing. It seemed that the tone of at least one article was that we should be alarmed about such a development. To hear about increasing oil inventory at today's prices was similar to hearing about some Missouri farmers who were putting corn into old barns and bins that had not been used for several years. It sounds like a typical production, price and storage capacity scenario.

Amidst all of the over analyzing about why the oil inventories were increasing, the fact that the storage facilities were built for that very purpose seemed to be ignored. They probably did not build those large storage tanks with the intent of only using half the capacity anymore than a rancher would buy a twenty ton bulk feed storage bin with the intent of never putting more than ten tons in it. Maybe some extra capacity is there as a contingency plan but that capacity was put there for a reason. Keeping an oil tank full at this time takes about the same investment as was required to keep it half full a year ago.

The risk of loss on the inventory investment is much lower at $45 per barrel than it was at $100 per barrel. In 2008 when oil prices surged to over $140 per barrel, some wholesalers did not fill their gasoline and diesel storage tanks simply because they had to stay on budget for the dollars put into inventory. Even though they maintained half or less as much inventory, many of them got caught with excess product on hand when the oil price crashed. At that point they had the choice of holding their inventory or selling it below cost.

As a consumer it is good to see adequate inventories of the things we use. The fact that somebody is storing the product shows some confidence that they believe that the market is not going to drop another fifty percent in the near future. With the increased production that we have seen in the U.S. in the past few years, combined with more than 50% decrease in price, it should be no surprise that oil inventories are increasing. One report from the International Energy Agency (EIA) stated that oil in storage is approaching the highest that it has been in eighty years. They did not mention the increase in population and the per person increase in consumption. The alarm that they seem to be sounding is that maximum storage capacity could be reached in the near future. Production and/or imports will be affected when the delivery points cannot handle any more product. Meat producers may remember the disaster that happened in the hog market a few years ago when the number of slaughter ready hogs exceeded the capacity of all the processing plants. Of course the big difference is that there is not a good method for storing market ready hogs.

Oil production in the U.S. for December 2014 was about 8.6M bbls/day compared to 7.4M in Dec. 2013, 6.5M in Dec. 2012 and 5.6M in Dec. 2011. Texas oil production hit a high point of about 2.6M barrels per day in August of 2014 and had decreased to about 2.3M barrels per day in December. Through November of 2014 the oil production in Texas had continued to increase at rates at least ten percent above the same month the previous year. In December that rate was less than one percent above the previous year. Regardless of the cause, production is no longer increasing. By comparison, North Dakota was still increasing the rate of production in December 2014 to about 1.25M bbls/day which is up from 927 thousand barrels per day for the same month last year.

The EIA reported that the non-OPEC oil supply in February 2015 was 1.4M bbls/day more than one year earlier. While the U.S. is still not producing enough oil to meet domestic consumption, the worldwide production appears to have exceeded consumption. That is being reflected in the price. West Texas Intermediate Crude was reported at $44.84 on March 14, 2015.

Baker-Hughes reported that the U.S. drilling rig count dropped by 67 last week. The rig count is about 37% below one year ago. That represents a bunch of jobs that came to an end. One farmer reported that he was trying to teach a laid-off oilfield worker to drive a tractor. The drilling industry and some supporting industries are hurting and at some point it will be seriously damaged. The drop in rig count does not include how many rigs were under construction and nearly ready to be put into service when the crunch hit. Same thing with the spare parts and expendables that had been ordered in anticipation of an increased demand for rigs. All of the analysts and economists can play with the numbers but one thing is for certain; with 1,125 rigs working in the U.S., this decline rate of 67 rigs per week becomes unsustainable in 17 weeks.

LW96...Oil About Ranching...Ag Teacher and Veterinarian

A little bit from both sides of the fence this week.

So far there does not appear to be a definitive answer for the question as to why gasoline prices are rising while crude oil prices are dropping and storage inventories are increasing. In Missouri, I saw where corn had been piled on the ground and covered with huge tarps. One pile was reported to consist of half a million bushels. Oil producers will have to find a different solution.

Many articles indicate that there is much consternation about what will happen when all of the oil storage facilities are filled to capacity. At the projected rate of filling storage facilities, we won't have to wait long to see if a glut occurs and results in gridlock. Some oil operators can close the valve with less risk of loss than the corn farmers would have if they just left the corn standing in the field. At least that oil can be stored in the ground as compared to on top of the ground.

On March 20, 2015 prices for West Texas Intermediate were $45.72 per barrel. The U.S. rig count dropped by another 56 rigs, down to a total of 1,069. Midland Reporter News reported that the Permian Basin rig count has dropped for 15 consecutive weeks from a high of 568 on Dec. 5, 2014 to 292 this week. By comparison, Canada had 389 rigs one year ago and now has 140 and only 30 of those are drilling for oil.

The gray horse was limping severely when he came up for feed one morning. It was an unusual limp and it was difficult to determine just which joint was affected. It was one of those strange occurrences that created many more questions than answers. Like many others, my typical last resort was to call the vet to see if he was available. The intent was not to have him try to diagnose the problem over the phone but he asked a few questions about how the horse was moving and if he was able to load in a trailer.

He said that I could bring the horse in and then made a comment as to how did I expect him to be able to figure out why the horse was limping if I couldn't figure it out. It was one of those statements that had a mixed message. The vet was giving me a compliment acknowledging my experience with horses. Later, I realized that it was not altogether a compliment but was also admonishment for not doing my homework and reminding me that if I brought a problem to him that he expected for me to analyze it so that I could be more definitive about the problem and also have some idea about a solution.

That was not the typical way for a veterinarian to respond to a customer and was probably not something that he was taught at the maroon and white vet school. Some time later I realized that in this case he was not just being my veterinarian. He had turned the clock back some thirty plus years and reverted back to again being my ag teacher and was telling me to study harder and encouraging me to diagnose the problem. When I was in high school, he was may ag teacher. We made a bunch of stock shows and other events. FFA was what made high school almost tolerable for me. Soon after I graduated from high school and started college, my ag teacher went to vet school. No doubt, I was one (and could, but won't, name many others) who had a strong influence on his decision to quit teaching.

Note that I did not say good influence, but STRONG influence. Upon completing vet school he returned home and was my veterinarian for many years.

As I've been going through my memory files, there are many situations to remind me that he really never quit being my teacher. Our visits usually consisted of us crossing trails at one place or another. Seems like we were both always in a hurry but took time to inquire about family and what adventure that either of us was working on. As always, our last conversation included him giving me encouragement about something. That was standard operating procedure for him to provide encouragement.

Some of you may remember the column where I told about field dressing a show lamb that ran into a fence and broke it's neck at the show barn when I was a senior in high school. This was the ag teacher who drove up and without asking any questions, simply stated that they weren't having a carcass contest. It's one of many memories where we laughed and made the best of a bad situation.

Friendships that span about fifty years are mighty special. We knew a lot about each others faults and weaknesses and sometimes we butted heads but through it all we remained friends and he remained my teacher to the end. He was a rare and special person who touched many people with his life. Many readers of this column knew him and we are all going to miss Jimmy Smith, DVM.

LW97...OIL ABOUT RANCHING...TIMING

Somewhere there must be a rancher who recently received a first royalty check. Someone who is outside the high activity area and never really expected to have a producing well on their property and has not watched the price of oil and the falling rig count. Looking at that first check with excitement and thankfulness without ever thinking about it being less than half what the checks were a year ago. There is no history with which to compare it, just that first check to enjoy. The amount of the check may be gauged by the incremental difference that it provides to make a land payment, pay for some medical expenses or making it possible to help someone in a special way. Even though there are not as many rigs working right now, somewhere there must be somebody who is looking at an oil check with a fresh perspective.

There were 1,048 drilling rigs working in the U.S. as of March 27, 2015 according the Baker-Hughes report. This is down 21 from the previous week. Compare this to Canada where 20 rigs were stacked out which reduced their total number to 120 drilling rigs at work. Not sure what is going on in Canada but a large percentage of rigs are being stacked. Some Canadian rigs and workers have been working in the U.S. for the past several years but it's never been clear as to how much of that is related to productivity and how much is to do with politics.

West Texas Intermediate crude was selling for $48.87 at the end of last week. There has been a slight rallying of oil prices along with the new battles going on in the mid-East. It is a reminder that our country is still not energy independent and that we still import more than one third of the oil that we consume. The surge of activity during the past few years has done much to increase domestic production and some of us are still trying to understand not only how the ups and downs happened so fast but why the oil prices crashed while we are still so far away from energy independence. Two things appear to stand out in the analysis: The world economies are very dependent upon oil for production of food and fiber, manufacturing and transportation. Even the countries so vehemently opposed to capitalism within their borders appear to use it extensively in international trade.

In spite of all the talk about politics and manipulation, there is evidence that fundamental supply and demand still have major impact on prices. A look back at petroleum consumption in the U.S. reveals an average of about 20.7 million barrels per day being consumed in 2005-2007 and then dropped by about twenty percent during the next five years. Domestic oil production increased by more than eighty percent during those same five years from 2007-2012 while imports dropped by about 25%.

A look back at oil prices shows an average of less than thirty dollars per barrel from 1994-2002. It more than tripled during the next decade and we recently witnessed a few years with prices over ninety dollars per barrel. Currently, oil is selling below the average of where it was ten years ago. Production, consumption and price all fluctuate. The only thing that seems to be consistent is how many predictions by various experts are not even close. One article December 2014, written by a bureaucrat in a state agency, who and which shall remain nameless, made the claim that oil prices would average just over $83 per barrel for 2015. Another headline this week predicted twenty years of low oil prices.

Some articles claimed that the decrease in consumption was based on the economy without giving mention of increases in efficiency. I know a lot of people who are now driving cars that they claim get more than thirty miles per gallon. From personal experience, the 2003 diesel pick-up has averaged (according to it's computer) about double the fuel mileage that was experienced with one that was purchased new in 1975 with a 454 gas engine. One cattle buyer told me a few years ago that he went to buy a new truck and told them that he didn't want one with all that new computerized stuff on it that he was hearing about. They informed him that all of their new trucks were computerized and it was not an option. Even though he didn't want to make the change to all the computerized new stuff, he said that in a short time he discovered that the efficiency of the new truck was enough that the savings in fuel was enough to make the truck payments. Regardless of what the numbers were behind the performance, he seemed very happy with the results from the new technology.

Along with new technology, there are some new sources of fuel that have been developed. Getting the "real true story" on ethanol is a problem. Every analysis seems to be from one bias or the other. To add further confusion, on a recent trip to Missouri, what appeared to be a diesel powered truck was witnessed hauling corn into an ethanol plant. It would have been interesting, but maybe not safe, to have asked them why they were using a diesel powered truck instead of one powered by ethanol?

LW98...Oil About Ranching...Methanol
(April 6, 2015)

Everybody wants lower fuel prices and we keep hoping that a phenomenal breakthrough will occur for a cheap, clean and unlimited supply of fuel. Frequently now we are seeing articles about falling fuel prices having a positive effect on farm and ranch economics. Recently an organization, which I respect and appreciate their work (but it is NOT an energy company), sent an email promoting a documentary about a new cheap fuel source. Not surprisingly, it turned out to be a mixture of science, propaganda and possibly a little re-writing of history.

The first flag went up during the first minute or so when the claim was made that the product was easy to make. They did not define "easy" but statements of something being "easy" seem to have a direct link to Murphy's Law. The film began promoting alcohol as a fuel source that was not hard to make and seemed to go back and forth between ethanol and methanol. At least they weren't claiming to have the "secret formula" and weren't trying to sell a membership, timeshare, or subscription. Some information was interesting and some just might, to be polite, be in need of just a little more research and fine tuning.

Not being a chemist (strong understatement unfortunately documented by college transcript) made it somewhat challenging to keep up with their fast talk about how to make methanol. Who can argue with the claim that the chemical symbol for methanol is CH_3OH? Then it was stated that carbon dioxide (CO_2) and water (H_2O) contain all of the elements that are needed to make methanol. Sounded like all you needed to do was gather it, mix it up and put it in the tank. Before having time to process the thought "carbonated water?" they had spun around and were extolling the virtues of methanol being used in race cars. Some claims were made about race drivers preferring methanol because it is less likely than gasoline to explode during a collision. Seems like a good enough reason to use it.

After making the pitch that if it's preferred by race drivers and that everybody should want it, the claim was made that the biggest reason we can't run it in most cars today is because of the way that the computer system is programmed. Then they sort of co-mingled information about ethanol and methanol and expounded on the number of "flex-fuel" vehicles on the road today and that with a few adjustments that methanol could be run in any vehicle today. So, we checked the operators manual for our very typical American made vehicle with a V8 gasoline engine and it clearly stated DO NOT use methanol in this vehicle. It may have something to do with the fact that methanol is used in solvents and that some seals and fittings are not compatible.

Curiosity demanded more research. A little web searching brought up a site providing information about the acclaimed largest producer of methanol in this country. Methanol is apparently a very widely used industrial chemical that is used in many products, including solvents, pesticides and to "denature" ethanol so that it will be poisonous to drink. Which brings up several interesting questions to ask someone at an ethanol plant whenever an invitation for a tour occurs.

One very interesting news article on the site said something about the company having purchased a methanol plant in South America. The plant was being sold because of a break down in negotiations with the neighboring country which had been supplying the natural gas which was the source fuel for making methanol. So much for the idea of easily mixing up carbon dioxide and water and putting it right in the tank. Also, the company was reportedly spending just over $500 Million to purchase and move the methanol plant. So much for it being cheap, unless factoring in that a new plant of the same configuration and capacity would cost about $1 Billion to construct.

Another problem with methanol is that by some accounts it takes 1.6 gallons of methanol to equal the same energy of one gallon of gasoline. Fuel tanks would need to be 60% larger and it would result in 60% more freight cost to get an equivalent amount of energy to the station where larger storage tanks would also be needed.

A quick check revealed a current wholesale price of $1.25 per gallon for methanol which would make it $2 energy equivalent to gasoline. Then add the thirty-eight cents per gallon tax (or would that be $.38 X 1.6?). That's a $2.38 cost before adding freight and any retail margin. At least it sounds like it is close to being competitive with gasoline but maybe just a little more work needs to be done.

An AP article told about a Swedish Ferry being converted to use methanol. The fuel conversion was being done at a cost of $24 Million. (Cheap?) Along with improved safety, there were some environmental benefits being claimed that in case of a spill the methanol breaks down quickly and harmlessly. Another article claimed that one of our Big Oil companies is working with a Chinese firm to enhance the process for converting methanol to gasoline. If methanol is so good, why would they want to CONVERT it? (My research is fuel for coffee shop discussion and does not meet scientific or journalistic requirements so all appropriate disclaimers apply.)

The week of April 3 closing price for West Texas Intermediate crude oil was about $49.55. Twenty more rigs were stacked out in the U.S. leaving 1,028 rigs working. Canada also went down by twenty taking their total working fleet to 100. Such is the reward for productive efficiency.

LW99...OIL ABOUT RANCHING...TEXAS RAILROAD COMMISSION

West Texas Intermediate crude oil was reported at $51.64 per barrel on April 10, 2015. The U.S. rig count dropped another 40 rigs to 988 which is 843 less than one year ago according to Baker-Hughes.

As a follow-up to a comment made several months ago about the consistency of an organization, it is pertinent to comment on it before something happens that will change it to inconsistent. At the risk of possibly being blamed for being the catalyst in the event that something does change, maybe a few comments and a compliment won't shake the structure. In this case the name does not match the activity.

A question that is often asked is "why is the state agency that is responsible for oil and gas regulations called the Texas Railroad Commission?" Having asked the same question about forty years ago and being told that it has always been that way did not really answer the question. A search of the history of the Texas Railroad Commission (TRRC) revealed that in 1917 the State Legislature declared that oil and gas pipelines were common carriers and gave the Railroad Commission jurisdiction over same. That was the first act to designate the Railroad Commission to administer the conservation laws regarding the production of oil and gas.

In 1919 Texas was the first state to pass a state wide rule regulating the spacing between wells. A note was included that this was done primarily to reduce fire hazards and to prevent damage to fresh water zones.

Then in 1920 the Legislature declared the production of oil and gas to be a public utility and assigned jurisdiction to the TRRC. In 1928 the first pro-ration order pertaining to the conservation statutes was issued by the commission and was first applied to the Hendrick Pool in Winkler County, (being the same field that was a leading benefactor for Hendrick Hospital in Abilene).

In 1930 a Proration Order was issued which limited the statewide production to 750,000 barrels per day and stated that is was based on the "reasonable market demand formula" (but no definition found for either reasonable or formula). This may have been the beginning step of government attempting to control the economics of supply and demand pertaining to oil and gas.

The TRRC is the agency that administers permits for oil and gas drilling. One of the absolutes for drilling wells in Texas is to have the TRRC permit in hand at the wellsite and calling the TRRC regarding the intent to drill. They are an advocate for ranchers and farmers and for all citizens through their responsibility to ensure the protection of fresh water zones. They are also responsible for regulations involving the plugging of wells that are being abandoned.

One experience a few years ago caused me to have a real appreciation of the RRC. Sometimes when drilling a well the underground formation does not cooperate. In some areas there are some formations that have a negative reaction to drilling fluids. These are often referred to as time sensitive shales, indicating that there is a limited window of time to drill the hole, pull the bit out, install the casing and pump cement. It is one of the many risks involved in drilling wells. Every well is different and just because field history indicates that there is a six day window of opportunity does not mean that Murphy's Law will not kick in on day four. It was one of those days and that ended up with pipe stuck in the hole and a fishing job that had gone past the point of no return.

While working with the RRC to get the approval and permit to plug and abandon the well, the fact struck me that it was a little after 7PM and that some individuals in a state government agency were working diligently to get the job done. With rig costs continuing and hole conditions deteriorating, it was a relief to be working with a group who was not restricted to working eight to five. Being the one who was in the hot seat between the oil company and the TRRC it was a relief that the TRRC employees understood what was happening and were working with us and telling us what we could do and not adding to the confusion with delays, denials and other dysfunctions. We were pumping cement to plug that well before daylight.

It is interesting that almost one hundred years later, the agency for oil and gas regulation is still called the Railroad Commission. There are many positive benefits about being consistent. It is nice to know "who's in charge" when dealing with regulations. Compare this to many other state and federal agencies and commissions that have come into being and have gone through various transformations, name changes, re-branding, re-purposing, centralizing, transforming, de-centralizing and building fancy buildings to enhance their image, clout or justification for being. Maybe there is something to be said for being underpaid and overworked that helps to prevent the previously referenced activities. If it ain't broke don't fix it. Here's hoping that they keep the name Texas Railroad Commission.

Page 248

Someday there will be another oil boom and they will be re-cycling a few old guys from the previous boom and they will need to know who to call.

LW100...Oil About Ranching...Trail Drivers

West Texas Intermediate crude oil was more than $56 per barrel on April 17, 2015. Thirty-four more rigs were stacked across the U.S. Many operators are hoping for oil to get a little higher so they can take a sigh of relief. One report on the oil bust emphasized that "nobody saw it coming". That's because it sneaks up on you, every time.

Sometimes we get what we want. Sort of. It just may take many years to realize it. It was one of those nights to really appreciate….a nice boring night in the oilfield. Age and experience had caused me to often say that I could enjoy some boring days in the oilfield and that I did not want any more excitement. The statement usually continued on that there had already been plenty of excitement and that there were more stories to tell than anybody wanted to hear, so no more excitement was needed. Many years ago, one co-worker had said that drilling foremen deal with days and days of boredom that are punctuated with moments of sheer terror. Adrenaline rushes no longer needed or appreciated. Compared to some other things, boring is good. Real good.

The rig was located northwest of Big Spring, TX in some of that sandy country with some rolling hills. You could see for miles from the rig floor and walkways. For some reason I was thinking about Red Steagall's poem or song about the cook always pointing the wagon tongue to the north when he set up camp so that he would know which direction to go in the morning, in case it was cloudy. That didn't pertain to us since we had maps, plats, GPS and cell phones and there was always somebody telling us where to go. There were eight or nine rigs working in the area that were visible from this vantage point. The farthest one was several miles away and would have been difficult for an untrained eye to identify.

Looking at the rig lights in the distance aroused some curiosity about what might be going on at some of the other rigs. Thinking about pointing the wagon tongue toward the North Star stirred up thoughts about some of the trail herds that possibly went through this area. The profile of the rig lights gave some perspective about the distance to the other rigs. A campfire for a neighboring trail herd would have been more difficult to determine the distance. There was a little more competition along with the curiosity among the trail herds and the traildrivers might have been more curious about what the other herds were doing. Finding the best water holes, (similar to having enough water trucks on call) getting there first before the water gets messed up, following the best grazing (having all the necessary supplies on location and verified for accuracy) and getting to the railhead first for the best market (maybe the herd was already contracted and the market not so much of a worry).

Having been accused of being born a hundred years too late and always having been drawn to the old west history plus an addiction to cattle and horses, the big cattle drives are something I wish that I could have done. The big exception would have been the preference to have had a self contained trailer with living quarters and all the modern conveniences! Those details notwithstanding, there was a strong probability of me fitting the trail driver profile more closely than the drilling foreman profile. There has always been that wish that I could have gone up the trail with a herd.

Then I thought about how the drilling business had taken me up many of those trails, plus a few others. From Big Spring to Rock Springs, Big Lake to Big Piney, Barstow to Biddle, Vealmoor to Vernal, Garden City TX to Garden City KS, Canadian TX to near the Canadian border, Guthrie to Gillette, Lovington to Labarge, Ft. Stockton to Ft. Smith, Pyote to Pinedale, Monahans to Medora, Elk City to Evanston, Coyanosa to Craig, Ozona to Baggs, Elida to Belle Creek, Rifle to Elk City and one well somewhere in Idaho but just can't remember where.

From seeing the desert bloom in the Pecos country to seeing wild horses in the Great Divide Basin and from the flatlands to the high mountains and burning hot to numbing cold. A bunch of real characters were met along the way. Maybe it wasn't the same as the trail drives, but it was a different time in history. Instead of a beef shortage up north there was an oil shortage everywhere. Just like the drovers who did not own the herds, I did not own the rigs, but we got to see a lot of magnificent country. Sometimes, without realizing it, we do sort of get what we want. If we are really fortunate we realize it in time to really appreciate it. Maybe I crossed your trail along the way.

LW101...OIL ABOUT RANCHING...RAILROAD COMMISSION NAME CHANGE

Fixing something that is not broke is quite possibly just a waste of good baling wire.

At the time of the writing of the previous article with some info about the Texas Railroad Commission and giving the opinion that when something is working as effectively as the TRRC that there is no need to fix it, this writer was not aware of the discussions taking place in the Texas Legislature about possibly changing the name. Just a little research will prove that the name of the agency provides absolutely no indication of any connection to the regulation of oil and gas exploration and production.

Who can argue with the logic of having the name of an entity containing some connection with the duties that are performed? But the question still remains, "Why does the name need to be changed?" We've just gone through one of the biggest oil booms that most of us have ever seen. The rapid rate of the growth of the industry and the Texas economy was a rare event. Would the oil boom have been bigger and better if the Texas Railroad Commission had been changed to the Texas Energy Commission? Really, how many wells did not get drilled simply because the people with the finances and technical expertise were unable to locate the agency which regulates and issues permits for oil and gas drilling? Now, for the flip side of the same question. If the name is changed how much confusion is going to be caused within the industry because of all the people who DID know who to call, suddenly will NOT know who to call?

No doubt the name is confusing to some people. Perhaps these individuals were already confused about life in general. Whose interest is being served to try to un-confuse these individuals? Where do they rank on the need to know list? Has it crossed anybody's mind that those who are confused by the name may also be members of the same group who thinks that oil and gas comes from the pump at the convenience store just like they believe that beef comes from the grocery store? Certain conditions can't be fixed.

Even if the legislature does change the name, they will not be able to change the long established habits of people. For an entire generation, people who work in the industry will continue to refer to it as the Railroad Commission. For proof, go to any rig in Texas and ask anybody on the crew where the TIW valve is located and they will point to an item located nearby in an easily accessible position. Ask them about the function of the TIW valve and they will explain that it is part of the safety equipment for well control situations and that it is a full opening ball valve that can be manually placed on the drill pipe or tubing in the event that fluid begins to flow. It can be screwed into the pipe while fluid is flowing through it (yes it will be messy) and then the valve can be closed to stop the flow. This is a first line of defense for preventing a blow-out. All of the workers on a rig are trained to know the function and location of this particular safety valve.

The people who need to use the TIW valve know what it is and how it works. Ask them why it is called a TIW valve and if they are under fifty they probably won't know. Ask them who manufactures the TIW valve and they will look at it to see whatever name is stenciled into the side of the tool. Ask them why it is called a TIW valve if it doesn't have those initials anywhere on it and they probably will not know unless some old guy has told them that the original or at least early and most prominent "full opening safety valve" was made by a company called Texas Iron Works. It's sort of like the trademarked name "Crescent" for an adjustable wrench. Somebody else may make an almost identical item, but the trademark name almost becomes generic at some point. When needed, it's not really important what name is used for the TIW valve. What matters is that those who need to know are the ones who will know where it is and how to use it.

As stated previously, there is nothing like changing the name, rebranding, developing a new mission statement, reorganizing, centralizing, de-centralizing and modernizing to give the appearance of having done something. Even if the Legislature of the Great State of Texas does change the name, that doesn't mean that it will not create more confusion than it solves. We will still say Railroad Commission. Old habits die hard.

Somebody might remind the group in Austin that nobody has ever been able to change (fix) the reporting of grain that is quoted in price per bushel even though it is weighed on a scale registering pounds.

If the legislature really wants to fix something, they should fix the way that royalty owners are taxed and how those taxes are appraised and collected. One consultant is currently available to assist, provided my day rate stays the same.

Meanwhile, the U.S. rig count dropped by 22 to 932 rigs currently working. In the past twelve months the number of working rigs has been reduced by 929. The party may not be over but it sure feels like somebody shot out half the lights. West Texas Intermediate Crude was selling for $57.15 on April 24, 2015.

LW102...OIL ABOUT RANCHING...PRODUCTION AND CONSUMPTION

A nationally televised farm report on May 3, 2014 reported prices received by producers were lower on grains, beef, pork and poultry. Looks like the oil drilling industry is not alone in suffering from improved efficiency and over production. The U.S. rig count, according to BakerHughes, dropped by 27 that same week to 905 working rigs compared to 1,854 one year ago. West Texas Intermediate crude oil was reported at $59.15.

Oil consumption in the United States remained in a narrow range between about 15.2 and 17.7 million barrels oil per day (bopd) showing a slight increase from 1980 through 1995. Domestic production remained relatively constant 1980-86 and then began a gradual decline going from 8.6M bopd in 1986 to a low of 5M bopd in 2008. These statistics came from the U.S. Energy Administration. A bar chart that paints a picture of what happened from 1980-2013 and can be viewed at http://www.indexmundi.com/energy.aspx?country=us .

Looking back, the chart provides a warning with the decreasing production going the opposite direction of the increase in consumption along about 1986. That was the year that domestic oil prices crashed all the way to about $9 per barrel for a while. Is it possible such a low (manipulated by foreign producers?) price encouraged consumption to increase? It may have been following the supply and demand. Domestic consumption for 1980-2013 peaked at 20.8M bopd in 2005 at which time domestic production was within 3% of the low for this period trending down to a low point of 5M bopd.

At the low point in U.S. production in 2008, we also saw the record high prices that surged above $140 per barrel. Some claim that those high prices were caused by speculators more than by supply and demand. When the bubble burst and oil dropped by a hundred dollars per barrel, the speculator theory looked much more like fact than fiction.

U.S. production for 2014 was 8.6M bopd with consumption at 19.0 and 2015 production is projected to be 9.2M bopd with consumption at 19.3M bopd. A huge reminder that we are only a little over half way to being energy independent.

When oil prices crashed in 1986, there were some who claimed that wind and solar energy research and development were going to be set back by ten to fifteen years because low oil prices shifted the economics. It was about fifteen years later when the big wind farm projects were under construction. The wind farm projects no longer draw the level of attention that they did just a few years ago. Seeing equipment staged in for project construction in a couple of places without having seen anything in the news about the projects was an indication that they may no longer be considered news.

One rancher told me that he had signed a lease with a wind energy company. There have been many discussions about whether a person would rather have wind energy or oil production. Usually it is not a matter of choice. There are a lot more places where the wind blows than where the oil grows. It's probably best to harvest that which is in season. The bank processes both types of royalty checks in the same manner. That wind energy lease that happened is more substantial than the oil lease that almost (but didn't) happen.

The following site of the U.S. Energy Information Administration provides some information about the source of the electrical power generated in the U.S.

http://www.eia.gov/tools/faqs/faq.cfm?id=427&t=3. It shows that coal is the leader with 39% of the production, followed by natural gas at 27%, nuclear 19%, hydro 6%, wind 4.4%, biomass 1.7%, petroleum 1%, solar 0.4%, geothermal 0.4%, other gases less than 1%. Drilling and fracking directly impact slightly more than one fourth of the energy source for electricity generation.

A little more research revealed ERCOT's numbers for Texas wind production at 10.6% of the supply for 2014 which was up from 9.9%

In 2013 and up from 6.2% in 2009. Another report claimed that at one specific hour the windmills were producing almost 39% of the power on the grid in Texas. That indicates that the average production for the year was 27% of the absolute maximum capability that was produced on the best wind day of the year. With wind energy producing only 4.4% of the electrical energy consumed in the United States it will take a while for it to become the major player. Contrary to some opinion, wind power is not providing much direct competition for the oil and gas industry at this point.

Beware of what statisticians, economists and reporters will do with numbers. Based on the way that some analysts mis-report cause and effect, they could make the claim that at my current rate of gain of one pound per year since graduation in 1973 that in another forty-two years I could be at the optimum weight for a professional steer wrestler. A little more research regarding age, athletic ability (lack of) and the fact that I've never felt a compelling need to jump off of a good quarter horse onto a rangy Corriente steer puts the possibility at zero. As always, do your own research and verify the numbers.

LW103...OIL ABOUT RANCHING...GREENER ON THE OTHER SIDE OF THE FENCE

About a year ago the oil boom was going strong and we were hearing from all directions (except this column) that it was going to last forever. A good friend called one night and stated that he had a grandson who had heard about the grass being greener on the other side of the fence and wanted to quit a good job in a non oil-boom area and move to the oilfield and get one of those high paying oilfield jobs. He wanted me to talk with him and give him some advice. I reminded this friend that the best advice that comes from my corner is to simply watch what I do and then do the opposite. There is nothing quite like having an aptitude for buying at the peak and selling at the low point.

Although being a witness to some of my endeavors, he persisted that I visit with the young man. This reminded me a little of another young man many years ago who stopped for a visit and told me that he was going to start riding bulls. Now this high adrenaline teenager had never ridden a milk pen calf or been bucked off a Shetland pony. Some people should get no closer to the bucking chutes than row eight in the grandstand. This kid was definitely in that category. Knowing better than to try and talk him out of his hormone induced idea for impressing girls, we just sat and talked about some of the finer (messier) points about straddling a bovine. The question as to whether anyone had told him how to get his hand free from the rope when he got hung up (emphasis on WHEN not IF) caused enough of a shocked look on his face to indicate that progress was being made in the right direction. Seems like nobody had told him how the hand hold in a bull rope could roll into a position so that the so-called safe wrap suddenly becomes an overhand knot. Just being matter of fact about the importance of knowing where the tail of the rope is and yanking it to get free immediately rises to the top of the priority list at such a time. He never had thought about that. Later on, it was learned that he had decided to devote his time and talents to some other endeavor. His parents never thanked me, but they probably never knew about the discussion.

The young man who was thinking about moving to the oil patch was not quite in the same predicament but probably just needed to have some questions answered or more likely needed some answers to some questions he had not thought to ask. Did he enjoy living where he lived? Yes. Was he excited about the probability of paying twice as much for house payments or rent? Never thought about payments being higher! Did he or his wife know anybody in the area three hundred miles away? No. Did they think that they would really like living in the desert? No. How often was he home at night? Almost every night since he'd been promoted out of the construction crew. Week-ends off? Usually. Holidays? Off for almost all of them, too. How many hours was he working per week and did he really want to work twice that many? Forty hours and didn't think anybody worked eighty. Had anybody offered him a job that paid what was rumored that he could make in the oilfield? No. Did he know that even though wages were good that "reality wages" were probably thirty to fifty percent less than "rumor" wages. Even though some of his skills would transfer over and aid him in learning faster, did he really want to start at the bottom and go through all the learning process? No, but hoped to start in a position somewhat equivalent to the industry where he was working. What was his contingency plan for when the oil boom can to a sudden end without warning? But they said it was going to last forever this time!

There was no intent to tell him what to do or what his decision should be. He simply needed more information. There is a tremendous amount of difference in desperately needing a job than quitting a good job to go in search of greener pastures.

He did not want to miss out on the oil boom but fortunately stayed where he was and missed the bust. He did not end up in the unfortunate group of last hired and first fired. The week ending May 8, 2015 saw another eight rigs put in mothballs in the U.S. and the end to several more jobs. West Texas Intermediate crude oil was bringing $59.39 per barrel and had crept a little above $60 during the week. One independent operator indicated that they could get by at these prices since they didn't have a big debt to service and had not gotten overextended and tried to grow too fast.

Speaking of greener pastures, it was solid green (and wet!) all the way from Crews, Texas to Chilicothe, Missouri when we made the trip about three weeks ago. Just a month earlier, we made a trip over the same road and saw where several miles of the Flint Hills had been burned. What a difference that a month can make. It sort of made me want to get out and graze. The recent trip was the first time that I can remember seeing green grass and wet conditions all the way. The grass was not greener on the other side of the fence for the entire trip. It was beautiful and green all the way. There are some areas in other places that are still dry, but there is one stretch for more than seven hundred miles where a bunch of people can be very thankful.

LW104...OIL ABOUT RANCHING...WESTERN HERITAGE 2015

Regardless of the location or event, it seems like the price of oil comes up in the discussion. Visiting with a small group of friends following the meal and meeting of the Southwestern Cattle Raisers Association during the Western Heritage Ranch Rodeo in Abilene, we laughed about how saving two dollars on fuel could free up a person to go spend twenty dollars on something else. Maybe that is the key to the multiplier effect that chambers of commerce and other promoters continue to advertise. The lower fuel prices may or may not have had any impact on attendance. A quick look at the parking lot indicated that most of the horses were hauled to the competition. There were so many trailers that it appeared that there may have been more horse trailers than horses at the event.

Even though the oil business has its own rich history, in more ways than one, it does not have the romantic history of the ranching industry. The petroleum organizations are mostly professional groups focused on a particular discipline. There are no "fun type" competitions to compare with the equine sports. I remember seeing a western poster many years that belonged to John Foster, who worked for Oliver Saddle shop for several years. The poster had a handwritten statement which claimed something like "The American Cowboy is the Greatest Cultural Common Denominator". I'm not positive that John was the originator of that saying, but it sounds like something he would say. You don't see cowboys dressing up like oilfield workers to go play on the week-ends. Nor do they dress up and act like lawyers, accountants or tech gurus.

The fascination with the western and ranching lifestyle is probably rooted much deeper in history than just the American Cowboy. All through history, the horse has played an important role. There is a lot of truth in the statement about how everyone, figuratively and literally, looks up to the individual mounted on a horse.

It is always interesting to see something that is truly successful. The Western Heritage has grown exponentially from that first ranch rodeo that took place in the horse barn thirty something years ago when there was no need to order tickets ahead of time and nobody thought about reserved seats. Very few events can grow in the size and scope of the Western Heritage, and thirty years later remain focused on their core values. The ranch rodeo competition has become a little more polished and it is obvious that a lot of planning and coordination is involved in putting on such a big production. The opportunity to listen to announcer Hadley Barrett do the opening ceremonies with emphasis on patriotism, faith and values is worth more than the price of the tickets.

The Texas and Southwestern Cattle Raisers Association (TSCRA) is a fascinating organization that is made up of, by and for cowboys that continues to operate on the basis of their original premise prevent cattle theft. The elite force of specially commissioned Texas Rangers paid for by the association, not by taxpayers, has such a reputation for investigating and prosecuting cattle and ranch related thefts that they are a major deterrent. That alone makes the association dues worthwhile. The fact that the scope of the organization has realized that all the so-called thieves aren't necessarily hiding in the brush has necessitated their involvement in lobbying. Having the TSCRA meeting during the Western Heritage is a natural fit but it still took some brilliant minds to put it together.

A recent report stated that the average age of cattle ranchers is sixty-five. Maybe if the teachers organizations had remained focused on their original values, similar to the TSCRA, they would not be witnessing so many teachers retiring as soon as they reach the minimum age and time of service requirements. More on that in another column.

There is a need in the oilfield for an organization similar to the cattle raisers association. Some big ranches where there is considerable oil field activity have printed pamphlets with all of their rules and regulations about what can and cannot occur on their property yet there is a very important item that none of them address. Maybe this is something where the cattle raisers associations need to be involved. It fits into the similar scenario of telling a soon to be married nephew that I would sell him some advice but I wasn't going to give him any of that free stuff like others were doing.

BakerHughes reported that the U.S. rig count dropped by 6, week ending May 15, 2015 leaving the 888 active rigs working in the U.S. compared to 1,861 rigs working same time last year. West Texas Intermediate Crude oil was reported at $59.69.

LW105...Oil About Ranching...Impact of Oil Prices. May 22, 2015

Two companies that have been major players in the recent oil boom and the not quite yet Cline Shale boom were reported to have each taken write-downs exceeding THREE BILLION DOLLARS on their investments. Not to be confused with the national debt and other government budgeting, this represents real equity from real investors. Yes, that is Billion with a "B".

Several articles have indicated that the recent oil boom was primarily financed by private equity investments and so called junk bonds. Some reports indicate that the financial disaster is being spread over a more diverse investment group than what we witnessed thirty plus years ago when some highly leveraged loans caused some bank failures and the dominoes tumbled for a while.

A few people are claiming that the bust has not had as much negative impact as they had anticipated in some of the communities in the most active oil exploration areas. Of course, major economic impact is like the definition of major surgery and all depends on how close you are to the knife. One area which is being impacted is the county budgets in some of the counties which rely on the taxes from oil and gas properties. The county treasurer in one nearby rural county with a relatively small population revealed that the valuations were down by fifty million dollars. Okay, somebody guessed wrong.

It is a mystery why this antiquated and somewhat dysfunctional (inaccurate) process of "appraisals" continues to be used for the basis of taxation. What is the advantage of using a once a year "professional guess" (as in paid guesser) to set the value for taxation? Compare it to the road tax that you pay at the gas pump every time you buy gas. How efficient would it be if your individual road taxes were based on somebody's guesstimate of how many miles that you might drive in the coming year and what might be your average mileage? And then be sent a bill for an annual tax for the amount of fuel which you MIGHT use. The benefit to the tax payer is that the pain would really be felt by writing out that once a year payment for the road tax.

LW106...OIL ABOUT RANCHING...DAMAGES & SITE CLEAN-UP

It is great to be an optimist and always hope for the best. However, experience teaches the value of preparing for the worst case scenario. There is no doubt that when oil prices dropped by more than fifty percent, cash flow was affected in a negative way for every oil producer . Some have deeper pockets to weather the storm while others may have been over extended with debt. To say that some severe budget cutting has taken place is probably an understatement. Any expenditure that can be put off will probably be put off indefinitely.

Many things may change from the beginning of a project to the end of the project. When it comes to location damages and site clean up at the end, the original good intentions may have been forgotten. The person who negotiated the lease will probably not be involved with the needed site reclamation which may happen months or years in the future. The lease may be sold multiple times and go through various operators. What is actually written in the original lease agreement about site restoration may only vaguely resemble what a landowner remembers from the conversation which occurred a long time ago with the lease agent.

Even with the best lawyers and best contracts, the possibility exists that the site will not be cleaned up and restored as promised. Sure, you've got a contract but if there is no "they" there, then "they" aren't going to do anything. The next to worst case scenario ends up being that you can't get blood out of a turnip. The worst case scenario is that you spend a lot on legal fees trying to get blood out of a turnip yet still have a site that needs to be cleaned and restored.

Most companies will probably try to perform site clean up and restoration in accordance with the contract. What if the lease is sold off to a company that goes under? Or what if they make an effort to clean it up and the grass that they planted during the dry spell never does come up? There is a high probability that the low bidder who does the site reclamation may not meet the high expectations of the landowner. It's a little late at that point to try to go back to square one and get everything right. Experience can be a tough but effective teacher. Even if there is no next time for the owner, maybe the experience can be passed along to the next generation.

If you are hosting some big event with lots of people out in your pasture for an indefinite period of time, you know going into in that you are probably going to have a mess to clean up when it's all over. That may be a good way to look at it when you are signing a lease agreement. As a former neighbor used to say; if he wanted something done his way, he probably better do it himself. He always clarified that he was not saying done the right way, but done his way. Planning ahead can prevent grief later on.

One way is to negotiate the payment for damages as being what you will have available for cleaning up the site in the worst case scenario. Simply dedicate those funds paid for damages to future site restoration efforts and be prepared to do it yourself. Then you can re-seed the area in the early spring instead of late summer when the contractor can get to it. Or if your needs change and you need the hard packed location for equipment storage or a hunting camp, you may not want to have the site restored. In that case you got paid for damages and then it worked out as an improvement.

Even if everything works out perfectly and the company restores the site to your highest hopes, you can be pleasantly surprised rather than dismally disappointed. Hopefully, you will not have to deal with that scenario. To again quote a favorite saying of an old friend, "Blessed is he who expecteth nothing for he shall not be disappointed."

The week ending May 29, 2015 saw another ten rigs stacked out in the U.S., taking the nation's rig count down to 875 working rigs, according to Baker-Hughes. West Texas Intermediate crude oil was quoted at $57.45. Oil companies are probably dealing with this price level about like ranchers adjusted to the twelve month feeding program during the drought. Although my time in the oil patch ended a few months sooner than I had planned, looking at green grass and the best spring we've had in many years has been a blessing. The grass being up may have something to do with my blood pressure being down.

LW107...OIL ABOUT RANCHING...PRODUCTION, CONSUMPTION JUNE 6, 2015

As the price of fuel goes down, consumption goes up and we are again witness to the economic fundamentals of supply and demand. The U.S. Energy Information Administration (E.I.A.) reports that consumers used 70,000 more barrels fuel per day in 2014 than in the previous year. Their forecast is that consumption will increase by 340,000 bpd in 2015 and another 70,000 bpd in 2016. The increases in efficiency in vehicles and equipment is not keeping pace with the consumer demand.

Crude oil has dropped almost fifty percent and prices at the pump have dropped about twenty-five percent. Ranchers and farmers have long understood the reality of selling everything that they produce at wholesale prices while paying retail for all purchases. The oil producers also identify with that scenario. The raw product may go down in price but taxes, insurance, repairs and maintenance seem to stick at their most recent high point.

Domestic producers appear to be adjusting to the lower prices and there is still a great deal of production work going on in the oil field even though the drilling industry has taken a big hit. This week the U.S. rig count dropped by 7 to 868. The International rig count went down 44 to 1,158. Notice that two-thirds of the drilling rigs in the world are working in the U.S. With rig numbers dropping almost everywhere, Canada is bucking the trend by putting 18 more rigs to work this week and bringing their total up to 116. Maybe some of the Canadians who had been working in Texas were ready to go home when the weather got hot. Weather and/or politics may have been the driving forces behind the increase in Canadian activity.

OPEC is reported to have the intent to maintain the status quo and keep production at about thirty million barrels per day. The desire to maintain current oil prices may be more about maintaining market share than maximizing returns. Trying to figure out what the OPEC countries are thinking is a bigger project than which most of us would want to participate. With all of the various factions and conflicts going on in the Mid-East it is intriguing that they are in agreement about their production targets. Who knows how much difference exists in operating costs and overhead from one country to another? Venezuela is reported to need $120 per barrel just to break even. With crude oil selling at less than half that, it would be a good case study regarding diminishing returns. It is doubtful that increased volume could fix their problem.

The E.I.A. reports that Hydrocarbon Gas Liquids (HGL)production dropped by100,000 bpd in 2014 and is projected to increase by 120,000 bpd in 2015 and add another 60,000 bpd in 2016 as new petrochemical plant capacity increases. Sometimes we focus so much on crude prices and production that the impact of natural gas being used to produce liquid fuel is overlooked.

The U.S. Liquid fuel production as reported by the E.I.A. (numbers in Million Barrels per Day) for 2014 showed Crude at 8.66, Natural Gas Liquids 2.96, Fuel Ethanol 0.94, and BioDiesel at 0.08 for a total average production of 12.64 MBD.

Consumption numbers report Gasoline at 8.92,

Distillate fuel oil (HGL) 4.01, Jet Fuel 1.47 for an average consumption of 19.03 MBD. Based on these numbers the U.S. is producing sixty-six percent of the fuel which it consumes. The E.I.A. predicts that the import share will continue to decline in 2016 to the lowest percentage of imports in forty-seven years. Keep in mind that is lowest percentage as compared to production and not necessarily the lowest volume.

The E.I.A. reports also included that HGL exports were 560,000 BPD in 2014 and are projected to increase to 1,000,000 BPD in 2016. How many people know that by law, crude oil cannot be exported from the U.S. but the HGL, processed from natural gas, can legally be exported? One of the rare cases where we are exporting a processed, value added, commodity rather than simply raw material. Do we ever think of those petrochemical plants as being manufacturers of products for export?

West Texas Intermediate Crude Oil was $58.88 per barrel on Friday, June 5. Natural Gas was $2.59 MCF.

LW108...Oil About Ranching...Noise

Listening to cows munch on grass is a soothing sound. Those of us who use the bovine powered yard trimming and fertilizer service should be recognized as being leaders in the all natural environmental movement. Sitting on the porch while watching and listening to the cows eat grass is a relaxing comparison to being around the constant sound of a drilling rig.

Drilling rigs are noisy. Some are worse than others. A minimum of three diesel and/or natural gas engines are running when the rig is running and the number of engines increases to a dozen or more depending on the size and complexity of the project. Basic rig power for hoisting and rotating is provided by two or three engines. There are also at least two pumps for circulating the drilling mud which flushes out the drilled cuttings. Various other generators, pumps and auxiliary equipment may be in operation at any time.

One of the benefits of the older "power rigs" as we call them is that the sound of the engines give signals as to what is happening. Everyone who has spent time working around a power rig has stories to tell about how a change in the sound of an engine got their attention. A rig engine may have the sound of handling an increased load because of increased torque from the bit or it may suddenly sound more relaxed because the load has decreased due to the drill string twisting off. Something like a plugged bit, change in formation or loss of returns may affect the load on the pump engines. Many of us learned to react to a change in the sound because we knew that something had happened.

Many years ago on one of those power rigs, I was catching some shut eye in the Chevy Hotel. On those fairly shallow wells we didn't have trailer houses for office and living quarters but maybe had a motel room some distance away where hopefully we could get by for a shower every two or three days and maybe sleep there occasionally. Seems like most of the sleeping was done in the car due to the need to be at the well site. Some change in the noise caused a quick wake up and it was time to pull on the boots and hit the ground running. Well running was against the rules even back then but by the time the second boot was on my vision was clear enough to see that the kelly was half-way down and not moving. That's a bad sign when the rig is supposed to be drilling, especially if it's in the infamous red-bed formation which is where we were at the time. Running up the steps of the rig, it was discovered that the entire night crew was asleep. Fortunately we got things to running quickly and were not stuck.

The absence of sound around a drilling rig can be more startling than many of the loud noises and things banging around. When all power is lost and everything suddenly becomes quiet it can wake up any drilling foreman who is lucky enough to be catching some sleep. All of the responsibility keeps the mind working and the sudden wake up from either silence or an unusual noise opens the mental file on a long list of possibilities.

The constant noise can be nerve wracking. Some of the newer electric rigs that are powered from diesel generators have some unusual sounds. Most of last year involved one of those that had sort of a whine or buzz that could be very irritating. That sound was normal for that equipment because that is the way it sounded when everything was running properly. Getting away from that rig made me really enjoy silence and soothing natural sounds.

We woke up early at a bed and breakfast in the small town of Jamesport, Missouri. Surprisingly, it was as quiet as being at home in the country. At daylight we heard the birds singing familiar tunes soon followed by the clip-clop sound of a Standardbred horse traveling at a nice gait while pulling a buggy. The smooth cadence of the hoof beats on the pavement fell easy on the ears and seemed to be in harmony with the singing of the birds. Buggies appear to be the preferred method of transportation in Jamesport. The people in buggies did not seem to be hurried or stressed out. Maybe it was because they weren't trying to text or talk on a cell phone while driving. The peaceful sound of the horses hooves on the street matched the pleasant contented looks of the passengers in the wagons.

For just a little while, it made me forget about the price of oil and the rig count. The week ending June 13, 2015 saw the U.S. rig count drop another 9 rigs according to BakerHughes who also showed West Texas Intermediate Crude oil selling for $59.96.

LW110...OIL ABOUT RANCHING...IRS

After what seems to be more than six months of a continuous downhill slide, the U.S. rig count was UP by two according to BakerHughes on June 26, 2014. West Texas Intermediate Crude was reported at $59.20 per barrel.

It was heartwarming to have several readers contact me when I missed getting a column in a few months ago. My response to blame it on the IRS was more fact than fiction. Regardless of how you are involved in the oil or ranching business, whether as a producer or consumer, taxes are probably a major issue. With the realization that this really can happen to anyone, maybe an overview of the experience will help someone else to be prepared, just in case.

In November, a letter arrived from the IRS informing me that I had been selected for a random compliance audit on my 2012 taxes. There were thirty-two designated line items for which they were requesting documentation and explanation. These items were scattered across Schedules A-F plus one or two more. The first call was to my tax preparer, a retired IRS agent, who I pay to keep me in compliance with the IRS. His opinion was that based on my income and the amount of taxes that paid in 2012, it made no sense to audit my return because there was not enough potential margin of error to be worth their time. That really made me wonder WHY is this audit happening. Surviving two accounting classes in college did not make me an accountant but did help create at least a working knowledge of accounting fundamentals and to fear an IRS audit.

One of the main problems with an accounting audit is that to reconcile a line item on a form, the entire form and all documentation must be reviewed for accuracy and proper documentation. One question for my tax preparer was that this had all the appearances of a fishing expedition. As explained to me, in a criminal audit they were limited to searching only the records directly involving the charges. However, a random audit was a different scenario and they can look at EVERYTHING.

Being much more familiar with the theory of Murphy's Law than Tax Law, the theory was about to be exercised again. For one thing, there was the timing. It was November and the pressing need was to be working on 2014 taxes and not going back to re-lick the 2012 calf! There was simply no time for it. Working full time as a drilling consultant and averaging more than eighty hours per week (documented) on the job site, along with paying substantial quarterly payments it seemed like they should have been more inclined to send a thank-you card than notice of an audit. I asked my tax guy if the IRS would do a 2014 audit instead so that I could take in all of what I needed to be working on. They could see the details, 2014 would be done and if they saw any problem, then we could go back and review 2012. No deal. To add to my suspicions and paranoia, a couple of weeks after the notice of the 2012 audit, a letter was received from the IRS which informed me that I owed almost four hundred dollars on my 2013 taxes. No details and no explanation as to what or why. I paid it immediately.

Nerves were already on edge along about November because of dropping oil prices. This old horse had been in the race a little too long and that 24 hour rig duty was taking a toll and there were already some signs of nearing physical and mental exhaustion. My attitude about the audit was not one of doing "all things in gladness" but rather being reminded that "the enemy comes to kill, steal and destroy."

It was nice to be scheduled for days off for Thanksgiving but all of my energy and much of my time was consumed by going through records to verify documentation of all activity. Even though I try to do everything correctly and abide by the rules, I am paranoid about the tax code. How could anyone trust the tax code? With TEN THOUSAND pages of rules and regulations which are often conflicting and/or ambiguous, how are we expected to comply when most of us have trouble with just the original ten rules which were carved in stone? I just about wore out a copy machine making (duplicate) copies of documents and receipts. I felt as though I had been falsely accused and was having to prove my innocence.

For a fee, my tax preparer agreed to be my representative with the IRS. After meeting with the IRS, my tax preparer informed me that the IRS agent stated that it looked like the IRS owed me some money due to overpayment. The IRS agent also stated that they wanted to see my cattle operation and the equipment involved in a small scale side-line business. I tried not to think about what the Constitution said about illegal search and seizure as I complied.

Several lessons were learned. There is no such thing as too much documentation. If a receipt applies to more than one of the tax schedules, make a copy and attach to the copy of the schedule which is kept on file. Make notes on receipts to explain what it is, where it was used and anything else that will eliminate having to rely on memory. More reasons than ever to support the FAIR TAX (H.R. 25) or some other form of flat tax.

    In May, I received a letter from the IRS informing that the audit had been completed and that the IRS determined that for 2012 I had overpaid. The IRS provided more than sixty pages of documentation and explanation mostly referencing various rules and regulations from the ten thousand pages of IRS code, as is it called. Not to be crude and talk about money, but the amount to be refunded was a little more than twice what I paid my tax preparer to be my representative with the IRS. (Sometimes it is better to hire someone else to do the talking.) Even though it resulted in learning that I had overpaid, it was not worth the effort. Some twenty-four hour rig duty or calving some heifers is a preferable alternative. Haven't seen it yet, but surely the refund check is in the mail.

LWIII...OIL ABOUT RANCHING...BREAK-EVEN

Some of us have been pencil whipped bad enough at one time to forever remain skeptical about the numbers that are presented to us. Questions continue to be asked about the break-even price for oil. The answers are not simple. The old saying "figures don't lie but liars figure" is a reminder that we need to know how the numbers were put together. Something that is probably more dangerous than "liars who figure" is one who believes that the data being used is accurate when it is not. Seeing a spreadsheet where a clueless bookkeeper had used the tax formula for "cost of goods sold" instead of the total cost of production to determine the break-even price of manufactured products can leave an impression to always want to know what goes into the figures.

How much can we really trust the numbers that we hear quoted about the break-even prices for oil that are reported by various countries? Who knows how they figure it? One of the numbers that we used to hear for comparison was the "lifting cost", that is what it was actually costing to get the oil from the ground to the nearby tanks. Looking at only the labor and maintenance costs and leaving out all of the overhead can change the numbers drastically. It's not difficult to figure that a flowing well has less lifting cost than one with a pumping unit powered by an electric motor.

If you talk to ten different oil producers, you might get ten different break-even estimates. Every extra layer of corporate overhead can add to the cost. If we can't determine the cost of production at home, how can we know what it is costing in other countries? Maybe somebody knows what all goes into figuring the break-even costs for some of the foreign countries. Do they have something similar to royalty payments? Maybe that's where they get the term "royal families", some of whom have reportedly been learning that there is no level of income which cannot be lived beyond.

One simple comparison is to look at royalty payments here at home and see how that may impact returns. One lease may have the stipulation for one-eighth royalty while another is required to pay one-forth royalty. If oil is sixty dollars per barrel, one eighth off the top leaves fifty-two dollars and fifty cents for the producing company, where the one paying one-fourth royalty will have only forty-five dollars per barrel. That's just a snapshot, but it's an example of how a twelve and a half percent difference in gross receipts may occur from one company to another.

While we may not know how other countries figure their break-even, it is very possible that they know much more about how those numbers are derived in the U.S. due to all of the readily available information in reports on publicly traded corporations. It's a reminder that the playing field is not level regarding the flow of information.

Recent reports regarding the break-even costs in major producing countries results in more questions than answers. There are some things that may, at some point, have a major impact on consumers. For instance, if it is true that Saudi Arabia requires ninety-two dollars per barrel to break even, how long are they going to be willing to sell oil at less than break-even prices just to maintain market share? How much comes off the top of that ninety-two dollars per barrel to pay the equivalent of royalty payments and is there any flexibility?

As consumers, we probably need to keep in mind that those countries who claim to be selling oil at less than break-even prices will not be content to sell at a loss for a long period. Based on some recent offers for royalty interest in the Permian Basin, it does appear that there are some investors who are betting for oil prices to rise in the future.

BakerHughes website reports West Texas Intermediate Crude oil at $54.97 on July 3, 2015. The International rig count was down by 44 while the U.S. rig count was up by 3 last week to 862. Considering the fact that we are now drilling wells in less than half the time we were a few years ago, there is still a lot of drilling taking place in this country. We probably should have seen it coming if we had really thought about how the drilling performance rate was increasing at the same time that all the new rigs were being built. It will be interesting to see how the next oil boom plays out. While we are waiting, I have an idea about what to do with some of those idle rigs.

LW112...Oil About Ranching   Maroon & Orange Rigs

The large number of drilling rigs sitting idle in various yards presents a significant challenge. Seems like we are always facing one challenge or another. Coming off of a strenuous two week hitch on a rig in the Rockies thirty plus years ago resulted in one of those rare encounters that provided an opportunity to have a conversation with a stranger who made a statement that is etched in my memory. After exchanging some pleasantries about the types of work in which each of us were involved, the stranger made a comment that other than the time spent eating and sleeping, almost all of our time was spent either being challenged or being entertained.

Through the years it seems that most activities do fit into one of those categories of being either "challenged or entertained". As the years go by, it seems that it was mostly those old challenges that now keep us entertained as we reminisce about them. When some old friends who rarely cross trails do bump into each other, it seems like the conversation always includes something about a really rough experience (that gets rougher every year) that was an extreme challenge for one or maybe both of them.

This challenge about what might be done with some of these idle drilling rigs gave birth to the idea that what we need is entertainment. One thing that was learned while working for big oil was to never present a problem without bringing along a possible solution. Another thing learned was that the difference between a not-so-good idea and a FANTASTIC idea was primarily dependent upon whose idea that it happened to be and about who gets the credit.

A few of us who knew we'd never get any credit for our ideas, occasionally enjoyed playing the game of dropping a bone to see if some big dog would pick it up and chew on it. When one of the top dogs took credit for not only finding, but inventing the bone, we had that satisfaction that is similar to roping something out in the pasture, in the brush, with that perfect loop and perfect timing that is so unbelievable that you can't tell anybody and just have to enjoy it and keep it to yourself. All of which leans toward the idea of no expectation to get any credit for the idea of what to do with some of those idle drilling rigs.

Unlike some western states, Texas did not give a majority of it's acreage to the federal government when it became a state. (Maybe some of those states can use their own variation of this idea.) However, a pretty good chunk of Texas was carved out and designated as University Land. That chunk being described as "pretty good" is an understatement considering that much of it sits on some very significant oil and gas deposits. It seems that the revenue is somehow divided up, maybe not necessarily equal, between a couple of institutions so famous that they are recognized without having their names called. Some reports indicate that they get considerable income from oil and gas royalties.

Those two universities could lease or buy some of these idle rigs and start drilling their own wells on the university land. We are talking about multiple teams competing against each other. Instead of settling for just royalty payments, they could get the whole kit and caboodle! Just picture a set of Maroon rigs on one side and a set of Orange rigs on the other. They may not compete against each other in football anymore, but this would create some real competition.

Every department could be involved. Engineering would probably want to run it (they always do) but if it is chaired in the athletic department as a competition it will get a lot more attention. Also, the athletic department may be the only one with enough budget to hire a great drilling manager (coach). Every department could be involved with their own applications of research and development. This could be an unprecedented track and field event. Even the psychology department could be involved and maybe find the answer to question about whether drilling rigs cause the certain behavior or is it the propensity for that behavior that is the cause for people to work on rigs. Instead of just field trips, they could spend entire semesters on site doing lab work and on the job training. This type of work study could eliminate student loans completely. Instead of a loan application, students would get a map with directions to their rig.

Somebody will probably claim that they had already ordered the maroon and orange paint and had this project on the drawing board long before this column was written. That's okay. That is how the game is played. With more than half the drilling fleet sitting idle and oil below $53, right now we could use some entertainment.

LW113...Oil About Ranching...Another Look at OPEC's Action

Being involved with cattle or oil is an effective method for avoiding boredom. There is always something going on and it seems like the more we try to understand all that is happening, the more confused we become. That is probably due in part to the information overload where we have too much information coming at us daily. Some of us keep trying to figure it out.

A friend sitting next to me at the auction where I sold half a dozen steers, asked me to figure the difference between the lightest and heaviest and see how much, if any, that the extra pounds were worth. The lightest weighed 530 and the heaviest showed 730 on the scales. The high selling steer was one of the two that weighed 730 pounds. The second highest selling animal weighed 530 and brought a sum that was only twenty-four dollars less than the one at the top. The lowest sale price was for a 715 pounder which was only fifteen pounds lighter than the heaviest but one-hundred and nine dollars lower on the check. Then there were two with a total tally of less than one dollar between them while they had a weight difference of ninety-five pounds. This scenario is really nothing new and reminds me of my first ag-economics lesson which was about the "hundred dollar calves". The situation was that 400 pound calves were bringing a quarter a pound and those at 500 pounds were bringing twenty cents and that there seemed to be a hundred dollar ceiling. I read that article, maybe in this paper, sometime while in elementary school. Thankfully, we made it over that hundred dollar barrier but it is still not an exact science.

Since we can't figure out the cattle price and weight question with the buyer and seller sitting in the same room, it really takes a great imagination to have any hope of figuring out the international oil market. With at least three major world events in play this past week involving Greece's debt, the Iranian nuclear deal and China's imploding stock market it was probably no surprise to anyone to see some volatility in the oil market. While we're watching to see if the lead OPEC producer is going to crank the choke to reduce production, the largest and fastest growing economy in the world stumbles while the European Union is growing ulcers about the Greek debt and it suddenly appears that Iran may be able to dump several million barrels of oil on the world market.

While most of the analysts have given the blame/credit for the drop in oil prices to a combination of the U.S. drilling and fracking industry and the attempt by OPEC to rein in the U.S. producers, one report by Breitbart had a different view of OPEC's attempt to control the world oil market. The article suggested that OPEC realized that by propping up the oil price to keep it above $70 per barrel that they had actually stimulated U.S. competition. The claim was put forth that they believed that the U.S. production would decrease if the price of oil decreased. Following that basic economic theory, the OPEC leaders may have started a "bear raid" on July 4, 2014. The report states that rather than falling, that the U.S. oil production increased from 8.6 mbd (million barrels per day) in July 2014 to 9.7 mbd in April of 2015.

The increased production by OPEC did follow the basic economics of reducing the price of oil but it did not decrease the U.S. production. The number of drilling rigs that were working did decrease dramatically and continually for twenty-nine weeks. Contrary to some incorrect perceptions, the number of drilling rigs working does not have a direct and immediate link to production. Drilling rigs, for the most part, do not produce oil during the drilling operation. When a drilling rig is shut down and stacked in the yard, that does not mean that a well has stopped producing. Basically, the drilling rig is used to drill the well, then the drilling rig moves out and a well service or completion rig (pulling unit) moves on to complete the process for bringing the well onto production.

Eventually, old wells will be depleted and production will decrease but for the short term it is possible that for every drilling rig that was idled, that there was at least one and possibly several well bores that were left behind and yet to be completed. With oil prices declining, this left a dilemma for many oil companies about the decision to continue to complete and produce these new wells or to wait until the price rebounds and do the completion then. With the decrease in drilling activity and oil prices, competition and price cutting probably occurred across all segments of the industry.

We don't really have to know what the individual companies were thinking or why they responded, whether by cutting back or staying on course. By looking at the continued increase in production for several months after prices fell, it was reported by the article that the intentions of opening the tap at OPEC has not resulted in the perceived intentions of reducing the U.S. production. If we can't figure out the price and weight questions on steers, we sure can't hope to know what domestic oil companies are thinking and are probably clueless as to the long range thinking and planning of

OPEC.

The one bit of good news for consumers, according to the report, is that the break-even price is now lower for U.S. producers. The bad news we can derive from the report is that if OPEC countries really are selling oil below their break-even price, they probably won't continue to do it forever.

West Texas Intermediate Crude oil closed at $50.89 and six more rigs were stacked out in the U.S. for the week ending 7-18-2015. Canadian rig count jumped 23 up to 192, according to BakerHughes.

LW114...OIL ABOUT RANCHING...HEAT STROKE

We have been thankful for the cool wet weather that lasted for several months and held off summer until the middle of July in our area. So far, the temperature has not hit one hundred degrees but may do it by the time this column is printed. We've seen many summers much hotter than this one. For instance, in 1978 when I began working in the production department for big oil between Knox City and Guthrie on the Bateman and Masterson Ranches. The temperature topped out around 114 degrees one day and it felt like an oven. Working outside, we tried to be cautious, limit our activity and drink plenty of water. It was a time to be cautious and not take any unnecessary risks.

We made it through the day okay and it was good to get back to town that afternoon. I saw a friend at a gas station. He was pulling a small open top stock trailer and said that he had shipped a bunch of cattle and that one heifer didn't look just right and was not put on the trucks and he was going to go out and pick up that heifer. Not being aware of anything better to do, offering to go along and help him seemed like a normal thing to do. What could go wrong?

Arriving at the pens, it appeared that the loading chute and portable panels used for loading the trucks had been removed. This left the heifer in a fairly large pen. After positioning the trailer at a gate in one corner we proceeded into the pen on foot to ease that heifer into the trailer. The heifer did not want to go into the trailer (an understatement!) The pen seemed to get larger with no sign of progress. We assessed the situation and determined that the heifer was suffering from a nylon deficiency. After tossing a loop on the heifer, we gently worked her up near the trailer, then I jumped into the trailer and quickly tied off so that the heifer was now at least close to the trailer and the two of us could hopefully encourage the heifer into the trailer without harm to any of the participants.

While tying the rope on the trailer, Guy hollered at me to be careful and not get too hot. Stepping out of the trailer, I told him that I was okay and just a little out of breath and that I would be okay. We pushed the heifer into the trailer and Guy told me that I was white as a sheet. I realized that I had totally stopped sweating. No water in the pick-up. Big mistake. The pick-up was not air conditioned or if it was the air conditioner was not working. Just down the road a short distance was a store. This was before it was common to have bottled water and sports drinks for rehydration. A sweetened carbonated beverage was not what is recommended but that's what was available. I got a coke and drank it while standing in front of an air-conditioner. After drinking about half of it, I broke a sweat with every sweat pore releasing water. It was such a relief.

At the time, I was unaware that I had just experienced a heat stroke. To me, it was just a case of getting a little too hot. Later on I learned how serious that could have been and to some extent it has affected me ever since. What they say about never fully getting over a heat stroke seems to be a fact. Several lessons were re-learned that day, including to not mess with cattle when it's over a hundred degrees and always, always have plenty of water available regardless of how short a distance or how little time you intend to spend out in the heat. Also, I was told that I should have gotten medical attention. Just a reminder that there are many things that are dangerous and being twenty-something and feeling invincible is high on the list. Maybe this reminder will prevent someone from getting into a similar situation and having heat related complications. It doesn't matter if your are working in the oil field or on a ranch, heat is dangerous.

There may be just as much sweating going on inside of some offices as there is outside with the current climate in the oilfield. BakerHughes Corp. provides the rig report and this week also reported that their revenue is down 33% from the prior year. Even though this is a substantial drop and has resulted in some deep cuts, it is evidence that there is still a lot of work going on in the oil field. For consumers, it is a good indicator that many of the companies in the oil and gas exploration are in it for the long haul. The rig report showed the U.S. rig count up by 19 and Canada up by 8 while the International count was down by 12. A report from Cushing, Oklahoma showed West Texas Intermediate Crude Oil spot price at $48.45 per barrel which added to the sweat factor on July 24, 2015.

LW115...OIL ABOUT RANCHING...TECHNOLOGY

The anniversary of the moon landing in 1969 went by with very little attention from the media. Just the slight mention of the moon voyage by American astronauts was a reminder of several technological advances and that two of the most successful government programs occurred in the sixties. Successful being defined as accomplishing what they set out to do. Many people thought that the screwworm eradication program had about as much possibility of success as putting a man on the moon. Thankfully, both programs far exceeded most expectations. At the time, it appeared that the accomplishments were major completions but now, in hindsight, it appears that these events were actually more of a starting point rather than a finish line for biological and technical developments.

By appearance, drilling rigs and space shuttles seem to have very little in common but many of the recent developments in drilling technology probably trace their roots to the space program. Most of the fundamental components of drilling rigs had their origins during the industrial revolution starting with steam engines and progressing to internal combustion engines. Advances in metallurgy to make gear reduction and power transfer units along with the development of the rotary drilling bit and drill pipe with threaded connections which facilitated drilling while pumping. Being able to pump the drilled cuttings from the well bore while drilling was a big improvement over the chisel and dip system of the original cable tool rigs.

The early visionaries had very limited research and development resources but a few industrious people developed some equipment that set the standard for decades. Standing on the platform of a drilling rig while making the ninety degree turn with about a three hundred feet radius with the computerized control system is a reminder of how far technology has advanced. It seems that the space program changed everything and catapulted us into the age of technology. Computers not only provide the control systems for drilling the wells but also provide the manufacturing systems for the hydraulic drilling motors and modern bits.

While discussing all of the technological advances, the younger guys were surprised to learn that pocket calculators were not in use until some time after my college graduation. Then they assume that it must have been a one room school with a dirt floor. My first pocket calculator was purchased on the way to the Exxon Drilling technology school in 1978. Since these were new gadgets for nearly all of us at that time, we were instructed as to the specific model to purchase. It was really a lot of fun and the calculations that it could do instantly were fascinating. Combined with a few mathematical formulas, that little calculator was quite an asset.

Some technology was not quickly accepted in the oilfield and that little calculator almost caused me to get hurt one day. Not long after completing the drilling technology school, my assignment was on a rig with a seasoned, stereotypical old school (maybe no-school would be more accurate) tool pusher who was about thirty years my senior and who was not happy to have to answer to another young guy who he thought was fresh out of school. My goal was to glean all of the knowledge that could be obtained from his experience regardless of his attitude and demeanor. His goal seemed to be to make my life miserable. He would constantly and emphatically remind me, "You learn this from EXPERIENCE and not from the (expletives deleted, and there were many) BOOK! It was an occasion where it was best to consider the source and not make any argument and just try to get along. After a few weeks of these constant reminders about learning it was getting more than a little old.

One day while in doghouse, the tool pusher asked if I had my Halliburton book, which is the basic oilfield reference manual containing various tables of dimensions and capacities. Answering that the book was down in the car, I then asked what he wanted to know. He said that he wanted to know how many barrels of fluid would be required to displace the capacity between the wellbore and the casing which we planned to put in the well. Pulling out the calculator and using a formula that I had learned, a few numbers were punched in and I turned the calculator to him and said, "That's how many barrels it will take." He looked at the calculator, then he looked at me and I tapped the calculator and quietly said, "Learned it from the book." Fire shot out of his eyes and for a minute I thought he would try to hit me but I held his gaze, then finally he started grinning. He was old school and realized that he had set himself up and had given me a good shot to meet him at his own game. After that, we got along really good.

Oil was about ten dollars a barrel back then. A lot of things have changed since then but it is fascinating that with all the changes, that basic calculator remains the same and I still carry one that has been in use for more than thirty years. Can't say the same about computers as I've lost count. One thing that hasn't changed is that we still consume more oil than we produce. West

Texas Intermediate Crude oil was quoted at $48.52 for the last day of July, 2015 and BakerHughes rig count showed the U.S. down by two, Canada up by 15 and International down by 12.

LW116...Oil About Ranching...Cold Weather, Warm Dog

It seems that almost everything that happens in the oilfield occurs when the weather is either below zero or above one hundred degrees. Maybe that's where the expressions originated about things being frozen in our memory or seared into memory. On these days that are hitting about a hundred and five, it is a good time to watch movies made in the snow and think about situations that were bone chilling cold.

My dog Frisco, a gift from Dennis and Donna Yadon in Alpine, started the dog days of August just after the middle of July. Frisco is not the world's greatest cow dog but what he may lack in talent is more than offset by his enthusiasm for the job and his comical personality. It seems that he blames me for the weather conditions. About three years ago we had an ice storm that coated everything and it was cold enough in Runnels County that I thought I was back on a drilling rig in Wyoming.

Regardless of the weather, Frisco is ready to go. When it's really cold he prefers to ride in the cab. So we take off to go feed a few cows. Frisco really likes to work cows and is quite accomplished at being a bovine antagonist. That means it is much safer for him to be restrained when I'm shaking some feed out of a sack. (Also it's a time to think about one of those trailer mounted cube feeders!) Leaving him in the pickup while pouring out some feed seemed like a good thing to do. The wind was blowing hard out of the north and the snow and ice made it seem even colder. Being properly dressed for the occasion, everything seemed to be in order while pouring out feed and listening to Frisco bark and bounce from side to side while inside the pick-up.

Upon reaching for the door handle, the discovery was made that the door was locked. It seems that Frisco, in his gymnastic endeavors, had hit the electric door locks and locked the door. Just imagine, a pick-up that is twelve years old and the electric locks still work. They don't make 'em like they used to. The contingency plan is to always carry a spare key in my billfold. But the habit is to never carry a billfold around the home place. So it was a long walk back to the house. Some of my realtor friends will probably pick up on the idea that this is a great way to make a small place in the country seem like a huge ranch. Just walk across it in bone chilling weather. It seems much larger.

Walking away with the wind to my back was not extremely bad. I was cold but had memories of being colder. Reliving those memories did not seem to warm my feet at all. After retrieving a key, the return walk facing the wind was even colder. As I approached the pick-up, Frisco was barking and bouncing around and was giving me the look. Where have you been? Why did you leave me in here with the heater running full blast? Don't you know it's HOT in here? What were you thinking? Why did you do this to me? He showed potential for being in a management position with some oil company by being able to place all of the blame on someone else while accepting zero responsibility for his own actions. Once the door was opened, he assured me that all was forgiven. We can learn a lot from a good dog. It would be fun to know if he remembers those cold days in February when he's laying in the mud under an apricot tree.

For some of us, it helps to think about some of those painfully cold days while we're sweating through August. Whether the power comes from petroleum, wind, solar, nuclear or coal, it is really nice to have adequate air conditioning.

It looks like the idea to rename the Texas Railroad Commission (TRRC) may have run out of steam during the recent legislative session. At least we still know which agency to go to for oil and gas information and regulation in Texas. Sure it would make sense for the name to say oil and gas, but it makes even more sense to not fix that which is not broke. Also, we'd miss the jokes about the engineers who run it and keep it on track. Also, it's good that we can still go to the same website for information. The TRRC's production report shows that Texas oil production topped out at almost 87M/bbls in December 2014. The first three months of 2015 were about ten percent above the same period last year. April was about one percent above the same time last year and May was about three percent less than a year ago. So it appears that the state production is either tapering off and/or being held back a little. Texas completions are down about 27 percent through the first six months. BakerHughes reports the U.S. rig count up by 10 to 884, Canada down by 7 to 208 and International down 28 to 1,118. West Texas Intermediate Crude Oil finished the first week of August 2015 at $43.87 per barrel. Have you noticed that diesel prices in some cases are now within a dime on unleaded gasoline where we were paying about a dollar extra in the not too distant past?

LW109...Oil About Ranching...Nepal

Not to make light of a huge catastrophe, but the question regarding the rig count in Nepal made an interesting point. Several searches have revealed no information about drilling activity in Nepal. Surely, if any drilling rigs were working in the area they would have been blamed for the earthquake and we would have heard about it in the news. There was a news item about an earthquake at another country where some mountain climbers were blamed for the occurrence because they were accused of taking, shall we say, immodest photos on top of the mountain. Seems like it is much easier and quicker to sell an idea based on lack of knowledge and/or superstition than it is to some basic research.

We don't have to own a degree in seismology or some other similar science to have some understanding as to why a house built on a mountainside goes downhill during a mudslide. Regardless of how many factors may be involved, it is rather obvious that the top layer of the ground shifted and relocated, taking everything downhill. It is easy to comprehend what happened when we can see the cause and effect. It becomes more complicated if something happens below the surface where we cannot see it.

It has become a matter of interest about the amount of true scientific data that is provided during an earthquake in one location while at other times when an accusation is made to blame an oil company, it seems that some basic data may be left out. Just making an observation, not an accusation, but some earthquake reports will mention some formations perhaps ten miles below the surface that scientists have been monitoring for decades and just a slight shift can send tremors to the surface. Other times, if there is or has been any drilling, fracking or fluid injection in the area, it seems that somebody is ready to connect the dots with a creative pen.

We don't need to know all of the details but it would be nice if they would at least report the depths of the formations that may have shifted. Just do the math and calculate the pressures. If something is going on ten miles below the surface, it is highly unlikely that any pressure injected at a depth of one or two miles is going to have an impact. Some will still argue that it "might could happen". If someone is going to argue against the laws of physics and claim that pressure does not follow the path of least resistance, then the facts will probably never matter to them.

One of the accused culprits in the news now is that injection wells are causing earthquakes. Maybe so. In most, but not all cases, injection wells are placing water that was produced with the oil then separated at surface, and is then is pumped back into the formation. Which is more logical, that a formation would be more stable with a portion of the fluid that has been pumped out to be replaced or simply left out to evaporate?

This is not an attempt to argue reservoir engineering technicalities. Rather it is that we should be provided with some basic supporting documentation regarding the engineering data on the subject.

Ranchers may tend the think that this is just an oil company problem but we need to be aware that somebody may attempt to connect the dots and start blaming landowners for leasing the property to the oil companies. When it boils down to the real agenda of control, there is probably no limit to the parties who may be blamed. It appears that we may need to be asking a lot more questions and requesting some accountability for the information that is being published. Again, I'm not saying that it is not possible that injection wells or dirty pictures can cause earthquakes. Far be it from me to accuse Hollywood of causing all those earthquakes because of their lack of modesty in movies. Fans of Hollywood will probably demand that they correlate the data before any such accusations are made. Oil companies should probably be given a similar benefit of the doubt.

BakerHughes reported that two more rigs were stacked out in the U.S. bringing the count down to 857 for the week ending June 19, 2015. This is 1,001 fewer than were operating one year ago. The Canadian rig count was up 9 to 136 which is 129 fewer than one year ago. The international rig count dropped by 44 to 1158, down 192 from last year. West Texas Intermediate Crude listed at $59.37.

RESOURCES

www.rrc.state.tx.us

www.bakerhughes.com

http://www.eia.gov (energy information administration)

www.recenter.tamu.edu

http://www.indexmundi.com/energy.aspx?country=us

http://www.eia.gov/tools/faqs/faq cfm?id=427&t=3

http://www.netl.doe.gov/File%20Library/Research/onsite%20research/publications/NETL-TRS-3-2014_Greene-County-Site_20140915_1_1.pdf.

An electronic version of this report can be found at: http://www.netl.doe.gov/research/on-site-research/publications/featured-technicalreports and https://edx.netl.doe.gov/ucr.

Some Common Oil Field Terms

Drilling Rig: Equipment that is used to drill a well. Most easily identified by the size of the derrick and auxiliary equipment.

Pulling Unit or Well Service Unit: Typically smaller and more mobile than the drilling rig. Typically used for replacing downhole pumps and or tubing in producing wells.

Pumping Unit: Typically a post and beam structure with either the rocking horse or grasshopper design. The pumping unit provides the reciprocal motion to function the downhole pump which is on the bottom of the tubing.

Company Man (also Drilling Consultant): On site project manager who represents the operating company that is providing the investment to drill the well. Responsible for planning and coordinating various contractors. Provides progress reports and daily cost to office. As some say, he is responsible for the money and the hole.

Tool Pusher of Rig Manager: Responsible for the rig and employees. Geologist: One who analyzes formations to pick the area to drill in search of oil or gas.

Land Man: Leasing agent that negotiates with property owners for leasing rights.

Land owner: Owns the surface of the land. May or may not also be royalty owner.

Royalty owner: Owner of mineral interest below the surface of the land. Typically paid a percentage of the production. May or may not also own surface rights.

Mud Engineer: Provides products and services pertaining to drilling fluids used in drilling the well.

Petroleum engineer: Planner and designer of equipment and processes.

Dirt Contractor: Provides the heavy equipment and personnel to construct the location and roads.

COMMON OIL FIELD ABBREVIATIONS

API: American Petroleum Institute (standards and guidelines)

BHP: Bottom Hole Pressure

BOP: Blow out preventer

BW: Brine water

DC: Drill collars

DP: Drill pipe

ECD: Equivalent circulating density

EMW: Equivalent Mud Weight

FCP: Final circulating pressure

FW: Fresh Water

H2S: Hydrogen Sulfide, Poison Gas

HP: Hydrostatic pressure

HWDP: Heavy weight drill pipe

ID: Inside Diameter

LP: Line pipe

MD: Measured Depth

MW: Mud weight

OD: Outside diameter

PIT: Pressure Integrity Test

PPG: Pounds per gallon

PSI: Pounds per square inch

SF: Safety factor

SICP: Shut in casing pressure
SIDP: Shut in drill pipe pressure
SPM: Strokes per minute
TBG: Tubing
TD: Total depth and/or target depth

NEEDIN MORE THAN RAIN

Lord we've been praying that this ole country would get real wet
Please forgive our impatience because it hasn't happened yet.
And speaking of forgiveness that's what we haven't asked for enough,
Help us to look to you and get our minds off this worldly stuff.

By the way that we've been talking and moaning and kicking the dirt
Looks like we think that we're the only ones who have ever been hurt.
So Lord, please forgive us for the way that we take on and complain
Help us to look into your Word and learn to understand the pain.

Thanks for putting up with us, a self-indulgent and ungrateful bunch,
While we sit in front of the air-conditioner and complain right after lunch!
We "suffer" in luxury in this bountiful land flowing with milk and honey
Oh Lord, please forgive us for worrying about things and money.

Maybe this is a reminder to count our blessings, good health, family and friends,
And we can just go on counting and the list never ends.
Help us to encourage one another to remember to always give you thanks,
Instead of worrying so much about those notes down at the banks!

In your Book, you tell us that all good and wonderful things are heaven sent
With this in mind, Lord, we come to you and of our sins we do repent.
Help us to concentrate on you Lord, and on the heavenly things above.
Cleanse us Lord, touch our hearts and fill us with your unending love.

Lord, you've placed us as stewards, over the crops, livestock and land,
So please watch over us and keep us in the palm of your hand.
Forgive us Lord for our selfish motives.   You know it's been awfully dry and hot
But your Word reminds us that we have not because we ask not.

So we come humbly before You and remember, Our God Reigns!
And we'll give you thanks for the gully washers that come with the rains
Help us to remember that you were there and that you heard our pleas
While we're fixing watergaps, there's more than one reason to be on our knees.

And Lord please be patient with us as we face another hot and dusty day
As we try our best Lord, help us to look to you for the rain for which we pray.
But most of all Lord, we need a spiritual rain for our dry and hardened heart
So we'll remember to gratefully say, "Thank You, Lord" when the raindrops start!
                               Justan Ole Sinner, saved by grace

THANKS FOR THE RAIN!

Lord I'm trying to think of a proper way to say thanks
The creek now has water up and over the banks
It's been a long time since we've had water in the tanks
Look upon my heart and know the sincerity of my thanks.

The long dry spell had a bunch of us on our knees
We're thankful that you answered our fervent pleas
Gave us a blessing, even more than the eye sees
A bountiful gift from you without any taxes or fees.

Now that it's really nice and green and sure plenty wet
Protect us, because now, maybe cattle are a good bet
So please watch over us, if a lesson we did not get
Before we think this is the best opportunity yet.

So Lord please protect us in our weakness and pride
And stay right here, up close and near to our side
Better yet, you ride point and be our Guide
Help us remember that You are with us on the ride.

Lord I want to thank you for all that you've done
This walking around in the mud has sure been fun
It won't be long 'til we look up and see the sun
Help us to properly direct our focus on your Son.

We're glad that now from the sun we no longer bake
Not knowing how much more that we could take.
We ask that you give those clouds another little shake
Give us a little more rain just to fill up that nice lake.

Thanks for all that you've done and are going to do
When we just couldn't go on, You pulled us through.
Even here in November some weeds and grass grew
We've really enjoyed the rain, the clouds and the dew

Lord we give you thanks for the gully washers and rains
You've put a lot of green on the hills and on the plains
As we look out it reminds us, that truly, Our God Reigns.
Thanks Lord and in our lives, we give you the reins.

By Justan Ole Sinner, SBG.   (public domain. LAUS DEO)

ABOUT THE AUTHOR

Dennis lives with his wife, Audine, who is a retired school teacher, in Runnels County, Texas on land that has been in continuous family ownership and operation since 1917. Their son, Roy, is a pilot and flight instructor. They raise cattle and have a few horses. Born in 1951 and growing up during the drought and taking care of cattle, sheep and angora goats provided a solid background in the livestock industry. A self-proclaimed carrier of the "equine mental syndrome" his cowboy credentials are listed as having learned to rope while doctoring livestock for screwworms and having scars acquired while shoeing his own horses.

When asked why he went to work in the oilfield some time after receiving a degree in Agriculture Economics, his response indicates that is where the "economics" became applicable. But he never sold his saddle. An opportunity to go into a training program with Exxon during the early stages of the oil boom in 1978 resulted in the opportunity for training to work as an on site Drilling Supervisor (company man) on contract drilling rigs. This resulted in eventually overseeing the drilling of wells in seven states. After moving back to the old home place after one oil bust, (never gave away his Halliburton book) he has returned to work as a drilling consultant on occasion for two more oil booms and busts. He says that he's not sure if he'll go back for the next oil boom. Never say never, again.